Praise for Jerry Dennis and Gle

"This writer-artist team shines a bright and lovely light on nature."
— *Los Angeles Times*

"Charming...informative...humorous...This wonderfully illustrated book will make heroes of parents and teachers, who will be able to explain nature's magic and the superstitions surrounding it."
—*El Paso Times*

"Vastly entertaining, valuable... Makes natural history so much fun the reader is sucked from paragraph to paragraph, page to page, chapter to chapter."
—*St. Louis Post-Dispatch*

"A perfect choice for adults and kids alike who want to discover more about how the world is put together... entertaining and fact-filled."
—*Houston Post*

"As leaves fall and the sky becomes more noticeable, you're likely to look towards the heavens and wonder at their mysteries...Author Jerry Dennis and illustrator Glenn Wolff address the questions with intelligence, wit and artistry."
—*Atlanta Constitution*

"A delightful book, both readable and informative—like the best of Hal Borland and Edwin Way Teale...You've many hours of pleasure waiting with *It's Raining Frogs and Fishes*."
—*Richmond Times-Dispatch*

A WALK
in the
ANIMAL
KINGDOM

Essays on Animals Wild and Tame

Also by JERRY DENNIS and GLENN WOLFF

The Bird in the Waterfall:
Exploring the Amazing World of Water

It's Raining Frogs and Fishes:
Four Seasons of Natural Phenomena and Oddities of the Sky

The Living Great Lakes:
Searching for the Heart of the Inland Seas

The Windward Shore:
A Winter on the Great Lakes

From a Wooden Canoe:
Reflections on Canoeing, Camping, and Classic Equipment

The River Home:
An Angler's Explorations

A Place on the Water:
An Angler's Reflections on Home

A WALK
in the
ANIMAL
KINGDOM

Essays on Animals Wild and Tame

JERRY DENNIS
drawings by
GLENN WOLFF

BIG MAPLE
PRESS

A WALK IN THE ANIMAL KINGDOM

ISBN-13: 978-1-940941-69-1

To Nick and Aaron
—J.D.

To Lillie and Sarah
—G.W.

CONTENTS

This is the third volume in a series of books about the wonders of nature that artist Glenn Wolff and I conceived the first time we met. Glenn and I had been a year apart in high school in Traverse City, Michigan, and although I remember him—he was the star of the art departments at Central High and at Northwestern Michigan College—we moved in different circles and didn't know each other. I lost track of him when he moved to Minnesota to study at the Minneapolis College of Art and Design, but grew aware of him again after he established himself in Manhattan as a freelance illustrator for *The New York Times*, *The Village Voice*, *Audubon*, *Sports Afield*, and other publications. My own early essays were starting to appear in some of those publications, and it wasn't unusual to see our work in the same issues.

Even after Glenn and his family returned to northern Michigan, we managed to avoid meeting. Finally one day our mutual friend, the artist Bernie Knox, pulled me to the telephone in her house. She placed the receiver in my hand and said, "Say hello to Glenn Wolff." I greeted him and suggested we meet for lunch at Stacey's Restaurant in downtown Traverse City. It was during that lunch that Glenn opened his sketchpad on the table and we began to outline books about natural phenomena of sky, water, and land.

Glenn knew an agent. She liked our idea for a series and pitched it to publishers. Soon we had a contract for the books that would become *It's Raining Frogs and Fishes*, about wonders of the sky, and *The Bird in the Waterfall*, about wonders of water.

The third book—the one you're now holding in your hands—began taking shape as Glenn and I wrote and illustrated a bimonthly column in *Wildlife Conservation Magazine*, the publication of The Wildlife Conservation Society and the Bronx Zoo. For nearly a decade we produced the "Natural Enquirer" column for the magazine, immersing ourselves in the fascinating world of wildlife behavior and the equally fascinating history of animal/human relationships. The staff at the magazine were a delight to work with and, more importantly, put us in touch with some of the world's prominent experts on wildlife, thus helping us to overcome, in part, at least, a rather glaring gap in our qualifications for doing the column. The truth is, we were not qualified at all. Neither Glenn nor I have backgrounds in biology beyond a few classes in high school and college. My education in the subject was worse than inadequate: in high school our class was so unruly that the instructor finally threw up his hands and surrendered. If my memory is correct he gave everyone a blanket C grade and spent the semester reading newspapers at his desk while the students romped through the classroom. I confess I did little romping myself. Instead I did my homework from other classes—not because I was a model student, but because I wanted to get those chores out of the way so that the moment the final bell rang I could rush off and go fishing. An inspiring science teacher could have probably nudged me to pursue a career in biology. My inspiration came instead from English teachers.

So although Glenn and I had little formal education in the natural sciences, we had been exploring the natural world with an almost scientific zeal all our lives. The field notes and sketches we've gathered since we were kids—and our determination to use canoes, backpacks, fishing rods, cameras, and binoculars to help gather them—recall those ages when amateur naturalists made important contributions to the knowledge of the world. Like backyard botanists and ornithologists of the eighteenth and nineteenth centuries, we are "amateurs" in the true sense of the word, with love for the subject our primary motivation. It is a motivation that spurred us to launch explorations to neighborhood woods and ponds when we were boys and continues to launch us on explorations today.

A biologist is trained to observe objectively, ignore personal emotions, and resist drawing conclusions until the evidence is complete. Amateur nature writers and artists go into the world to satisfy their curiosity and collect memories. For us, subjective experience has always been as important as objective observation. Noticing our own and other people's responses to nature is paramount because part of our work is to cultivate a state of sustained wonder as we seek clues to why we're on this fecund planet and how we should conduct ourselves during our stay. If some of the clues come from the behavior of ants in a colony or trout in a creek, so be it. Our job is to seek knowledge wherever we can.

Many of us remember our early encounters with animals other than humans. A dog, a cat, a wild bird on the windowsill—here was something astonishing, vivid, and alive. We might remember a feeling of strangeness in the presence of this "other" that was somehow both alien and kindred. It might have awakened an awareness that all living things are somehow connected. It might have been among our first intuitions of the fundamental mystery of life.

If we're lucky, those senses of mystery and strangeness never leave us, and in fact, only grow stronger and more nuanced as we explore the world and witness for ourselves the almost unimaginable abundance and diversity of things in the universe. If we lose those senses—and we all do, at least periodically—it's a relief to know that the loss is not irreversible and that they and our natural curiosity can be awakened in a moment.

Glenn and I were fortunate as children to have parents, teachers, and friends who encouraged us to explore the world and indulge our interests. In turn, we set out to teach our own children that being explorers is a worthy and honorable aspiration, and that an explorer does not necessarily have to travel to Antarctica or the Amazon. Wild places and an abundance of wildlife are everywhere, even in the busiest cities. There's a virtually endless number of them in our own backyards, beneath the night sky, in every park, woods, meadow, creek, and pond. All anyone needs to discover the wonders of the world is an inquisitive eye and a willingness to look.

We hope this book will in some small way be of help.

PART I

ANIMALS IN OUR LIVES

1
BELLYING UP TO THE WORLD

We want to reach the heart of the world, but first must know the surface. The problem is, there's no end to the surface.

When my sons were young they led me to amazing new places I had never thought to visit. Aaron, at four, said, "Dad, you're a kid in your brain and I'm a man." He collected seashells, old coins, basketball cards, and feathers, attaching deep and equal value to each, ready at any moment to abandon them all. One afternoon, as we walked in the meadow near our home, he watched fascinated as hundreds of starlings passed overhead in streaming, switching undulations, like a river of birds. Brimming with mission, I explained what they were doing, and why. I was in teacher mode, trying to share the information I was sure he would need to find his way in life. But he wasn't listening. He stretched out in the grass and crawled, following the trails of beetles and meadow voles, already immersed in some private immensity.

I followed him. I ruined the knees on my Dockers but, by God, I got down in the dirt with my son and became lost. And while I was there, happily nosing around among creatures I hadn't paid attention to in years, it occurred to me what an enormous kingdom there is among the grass stems and spider holes. I knew then what the nineteenth-century zoologist and geologist Louis Agassiz meant when he said, "I spent the summer traveling. I got halfway across my back yard."

Myrmecologists take note: My sons in their backyard travels have devised an effective technique for observing the foraging behavior of ants. Begin by placing half a teaspoon of granulated sugar in your mouth and swish it around to stimulate the production of saliva. Allow the solution to linger a few seconds on your tongue (especially near the tip, where, as three-year-old Nick explained, the taste "bugs" are most receptive), then with careful aim allow a drop of richly sugared saliva to fall to the ground, ideally in the path of a solitary ant. In our yard, the best ants for the purpose are the tiny red ones that have demonstrated their love of sweets by colonizing our kitchen. Their single-file trade route leads around the perimeter of the floor, up a wall, across the counter, and to the back of a cupboard where there's a ruptured bag of jelly beans left over from Easter.

Aaron, while mastering the saliva/sugar technique, noted that it takes a while for the scout who discovers the bounty to rush back to camp with the news and return with a company of workers. He noted also that the workers seem to follow a scent trail laid down by the scout but don't follow it unerringly. There is a certain amount of weaving and crisscrossing involved, reminiscent of the way a river in a delta divides into braided channels, as individual ants lose the trail then pick it up again and are followed by others who digress from the secondary trail, and so on. Eventually the ants create a wide, well traveled highway over the shortest practicable route from nest to food source. Soon a line of workers is busy transporting the dissolved sugar back to camp a bellyful at a time.

Once you start noticing the little worlds around you, there's no end to them. One spring the boys and I became interested in a tiny reservoir of water we found in the crotch of one of our yard maples. It was early

April, still cold enough to harbor a few patches of snow on north-facing slopes and too early for the black flies and mosquitoes that in a few weeks would be on the wing and on the hunt. The only insects we had seen until then were the small, pale-colored moths that emerge from leaf litter as soon as the snow is gone, before the insect-eating birds return to spoil the party. The boys and I peered into the cavity in the crotch of the maple and saw a glint of water deep inside. We inserted the nozzle of a squeeze-bulb device designed to draw samples of antifreeze from car radiators and drew out a half-pint of murky, odorous water, emptied it into a jar, and carried it inside the house. We placed the jar on the windowsill in the kitchen and waited for the sediment to settle. Soon we could see dozens of minute, nearly microscopic larvae wriggling in the water.

Within a few days the larvae had grown to an eighth-inch in length and were suspended head down from the surface of the water like slender bats hanging from the roof of a cavern. We noticed they were sensitive to shadows and vibrations: Pass your hand over the jar or tap it with a finger and the larvae would panic and begin frantically flexing their bodies. Nick was enchanted. He was convinced that we had discovered a new species and wondered if we could call a scientific hotline of some sort, register our discovery, and make taxonomic history.

Marston Bates, in *The Forest and the Seas*, talks about insects that have colonized the pools of water in "rot holes" in trees in South American rainforests and others that live their entire lives in the rainwater trapped among the leaves in bromeliad plants. He also describes a species of North American mosquito that deposits its eggs only in the reservoirs of water inside Venus flycatchers. Life sprouts anywhere it can— *everywhere* it can. Ecosystems—communities of interacting plants and animals and the environments they live in—are large or tiny, remote or close-at-hand. Within each community is a food chain of producers and consumers dependent upon one another. If the community is complex, as it almost always is, the food chain is more properly known as a food web. Countless complex dramas take place every moment in the hollows between the nodes of bamboo stalks, within the fruits of fig trees, and in our own backyards.

My half-educated guess was that our tree-hole wrigglers were the larvae of midges, those tiny harmless Diptera you see on spring and summer afternoons hovering in clouds above the ground or water. They often swarm in beams of sunlight, where they catch rides on subtle thermal currents. Entomologists have discovered that each swarm maintains a semi-permanent position near a "swarm marker" such as a tree branch or a patch of ground vegetation. Picking out a spatial locator apparently ensures that males and females congregate close enough to one another to increase their chances of meeting and mating.

While our larvae grew in their jar on the windowsill, we spent a lot of time outside observing the midges that gathered in swarms of thousands in our yard. They suspended in the air as if tethered to invisible cables to the ground, but when we walked among them they exhibited some of the same defensive alertness as the larvae in the jar. They moved out of our way, closing in behind us, careful to avoid contact but always quick to return to their hovering formations.

Meanwhile, our captive larvae fed on microorganisms in the surface film while breathing through miniscule snorkels, and grew to a quarter-inch in length. I was a bit of a hero in Nick's eyes, at least until the first of the larvae changed to pupae and metamorphosed into adult mosquitoes rather than midges. Mosquitoes are Diptera also, and are closely related to midges, but that's like comparing piranha to goldfish. Our neighborhood is infested every summer with small fast-flying mosquitoes the boys call "kamikazes" because they attack so viciously and apparently have no fear of dying. Now we know they hatch from tree holes. It's worth noting that they attack just as viciously indoors as out.

My sons have always been very good at reminding me how tiresome it can be to fill one's head with trivia. They didn't care a lick about the taxonomy of the mosquitoes in our house or of the tiny crustacean we found scrabbling among the pebbles at the beach. They wanted to know what it *is*, not what it is called. The goal, they reminded me, is to keep our eyes open and become one who notices and appreciates the bountifulness of the world. When they carried home bird's nests and owl pellets, wounded dragonflies and the dried claws of crayfish, it was pure booty. For a kid, observing and collecting are inseparable activities.

Those activities can be practiced year-around, but summer is the high season for low-level observations. Early on a summer day, when you kneel in wet grass and start searching, you become an explorer in exotic lands. A backyard, it turns out, can be as engaging as a rainforest. Within that fragrant jungle of weeds and grasses is an enormously varied biota of animals. Beetles lumber past in slow and clumsy gait. Leafhoppers poise on a leaf tip, then, at the first hint of danger, fling themselves into the air. Wolf spiders stalk, pause without moving for minutes at a time, then rush forward at terrible speed.

When adults explore the world at kid-level we're reminded that life thrives in such variety and complexity that we'll probably never be done cataloguing it. Also, and perhaps more importantly, we teach our children by example that it's okay to appreciate nature—that it is not just child's stuff.

In our age of instant entertainment and easy indoor diversions, children sometimes need to be encouraged to go outside. With a little nudging they'll explore the backyard in the old-fashioned, down-and-dirty way, with grubby fingers and muddy knees, carrying a fruit jar, a magnifying glass, and a butterfly net fashioned from cheesecloth and a coat hanger. Belly up to the world with a kid and you can form a bond for life. You might end up with a house full of mosquitoes, but surely that's a small price to pay.

Lammergeier

2
PERSONALLY SPEAKING

Much of my childhood was shared with a shaggy, black, cocker-spanielish mongrel named Menace ("Menace the Dennis"), who constantly astonished my family with his wit and charm. Menace knew precisely what time the school bus was due each day and would trot to the end of our road ten minutes before it arrived and wait for my brother and me. When we stepped off the bus he could tell at a glance what kind of day we had had and was instantly sympathetic. If we were happy, he was happy; if we were in pain, he was in pain. If Rick or I took off for home at a run, he gave a short, happy bark and ran after us, nipping at our pant legs. And when we fell tumbling in the grass he stood over us, grinning.

Because Menace shed copiously, my mother insisted he sleep in an insulated doghouse in the garage. On cold winter days he would come to the front of the house, sit on top of the picnic table on the porch, where we could not avoid seeing him through the kitchen window, and raise one paw in the air and whimper. The paw was not injured—if he heard the back door open he would streak around the house at full speed, thinking he was being invited inside—but he had learned once that such a display could inspire compassion and he never forgot the lesson.

Menace could grimace, sulk, sneer, smile, and chuckle, and I'm sure he knew how it felt to be contrite, joyful, melancholy, jealous, sympathetic, bored, and embarrassed. He had one of the keenest, most clearly defined personalities of any animal I have ever known.

This all sounds, I know, like the ramblings of a typical dog lover. It's also clearly anthropomorphic—a projection of human characteristics on non-human subjects—and in scientific circles would be rejected outright as subjective and sentimental. Yet it's a description millions of people would understand and accept as true.

The tendency to see human qualities in non-human creatures is so deeply ingrained in us that we seldom object when it pops up in daily life. Never mind that Bugs Bunny exhibits no rabbitlike qualities or that Garfield doesn't have a feline bone in his body. Those guys talk, sing, dance, and *feel* like people, and nobody questions the premise. It's an old habit.

For thousands of years we have turned to allegories and fables that dress animals in human garb to teach ourselves moral lessons. Along the way, we've come to think of animals as possessing stereotypical characteristics. The ass is stupid, the bee and ant are industrious, the owl wise, the lion noble, the dove gentle, the fox cunning. Those qualities appear in the earliest zoological texts and with great frequency in the bestiaries of the Middle Ages, where animals were used to illustrate ethical values and Christian doctrine. In bestiaries the hedgehog was described as a paragon of family responsibility: "The hedgehog has a kind of prudence for when the grapes fall from the vine, it rolls upside down on the bunch, and so brings it back to its young." It earned this virtue not because anyone had ever seen a hedgehog spear grapes and carry them to its offspring but because legends about that behavior supported a behavior that needed promoting.

Beginning in the seventeenth century with Descartes' view of animals as machines, and especially around the turn of the twentieth century, when behavioral psychology gained prominence, anthropomorphism was increasingly rejected as being antithetical to objective scientific observation. Biologists who a few decades earlier had been inspired by Darwin's assertion that we are animals ourselves and had set out to study other species for evidence of thoughts and emotions, suddenly swung to the other extreme and began assuming that animals could not think, had no awareness of their actions, and were without what we call, among humans, personality. They were considered little more than mechanical systems. Push a button, pull a lever, and a predictable action resulted. Chickadees became tiny feathered robots.

But the hunger for animal stories did not diminish, as Walt Disney discovered when Mickey Mouse, Bambi, and Dumbo were accepted as readily as Chanticleer and Reynard had been centuries before. We continue to feel warmest toward creatures that remind us of ourselves. We're enchanted by the raccoon's facility with its "hands" and with the bandit mask which seems so appropriate on what we usually think of as a mischievous garden-raider. We coo over the cuddly-looking koala and forget the nasty bite we might get if we attempted to hug the little marsupial. We watch the antics of monkeys and are reminded of energetic children. We admire the proud, fierce visage of a bald eagle.

In the 1930s, '40s, and '50s, biologists discovered that studying wildlife in natural settings offered startling insights into their behavior. Ethology, championed by researchers like Konrad Lorenz and Niko Tinbergen, reawakened interest in old questions about animal thinking, emotions, and personality, and mild anthropomorphism was seen as an acceptable way to describe what was learned. Their research and conclusions helped immensely to provide a more realistic, more naturalistic view of animal personalities. Some lapses were bound to occur, of course. As late as 1961, an eminent British naturalist described a close encounter with a lammergeier, a vulture found from southern Europe to Tibet, by claiming the bird possessed "sinister scarlet eyes and the look of greedy anticipation on his satanic bearded face...that evil disappointed bird kept his eyes on me, hoping for my bones..."

The more common forms of anthropomorphism are usually quite harmless. Often they're little more than literary devices or stylistic flourishes. Arthur Cleveland Bent's prose portraits of birds, for example, sound dated to our ears, yet can still make the birds seem alive. His description of the cedar waxwing, in *Life Histories of North American Wagtails, Shrikes, Vireos, and Their Allies* (1950), entertains while elucidating valid observations of the bird's behavior: "When we become well acquainted with the waxwing we look upon him as the perfect gentleman of the bird world. There is in him a refinement of deportment and dress; his voice is gentle and subdued; he is quiet and dignified in manner, sociable, never quarrelsome, and into one of his habits, that of sharing food with his companions, we may read, without too much stress of imagination, the quality of politeness, almost unselfishness, very rare, almost unheard of, in the animal kingdom."

A behavior characteristic to a species, such as a waxwing sharing food with others in its group, does not give an individual "personality." Personality is the totality of qualities unique to an individual. Even the most scientific-minded biologists, naturalists, zoo-keepers, and pet owners have noticed personalities in the animals they become familiar with. Konrad Lorenz's jackdaws, Jane Goodall's chimpanzees, Ken Armitage's yellow-bellied marmots—the list is long. A wonderful example is Joy Adamson's trio of orphaned lion cubs in *Born Free*: "Within a few days the cubs had settled down and were everybody's pets.... Even at this age each had a definite character. The 'Big One' had a benevolent superiority and was generous toward the others. The second was a clown, always laughing and spanking her milk bottle with both her front paws as she drank, her eyes closed in bliss....The third cub was the weakling in size, but the pluckiest in spirit. She pioneered all around, and was always sent by the others to reconnoiter when something looked suspicious to them. I called her Elsa, because she reminded me of someone of that name."

Some degree of anthropomorphism might be our best hope of intuiting what it feels like to be a nonhuman, sentient creature on earth.

Anyone who has observed a litter of lion cubs tumbling over one another, river otters sliding down a snow-covered bank, or a dog playing with a child has probably abandoned the notion that animals are motivated solely by mechanisms selected for survival and reproduction. Who can blame us for imagining that they experience emotions and sensations— "feelings"—very much like our own?

JUMPING SPIDER

BLACK WIDOW

TARANTULA

CALIFORNIA TRAPDOOR SPIDER

ARGYRONETA AQUATICA

3
ALONG CAME A SPIDER...

Our house is infested with spiders. I don't mind, not much anyway, but for years my wife and sons considered it a calamity. Nearly every day I was summoned to do the manly thing and dispose of the intruders. I nudged them into jars and released them outside, though my family would have been happier if I had employed more permanent measures—put my foot down firmly on the subject of spiders in the house.

When it comes to arachnids I'm like many people, curious but sometimes a little uneasy. I'm interested in the artistry of an orb weaver, the cunning efficiency of a wolf spider on the hunt, the acrobatics of a jumping spider. I'm intrigued enough to now and then get down on my knees in the garden to watch the spider dramas going on there. But if some evening I'm on the couch reading and glance down to see a many-legged hairy thing with fangs running across my chest, I'm on my feet in an instant, book flying across the room like a panicked bird. I can't help it. I'm interested in spiders, I admire them, but I would prefer they not crawl on me.

Even many people who are genuinely afraid of spiders will admit a grudging admiration for them. And it's good they do, for spiders are here to stay and they are plentiful. More than 40,000 species have been identified, with new ones being discovered almost daily. A typical acre of meadow, field, or woods almost anywhere on the planet can contain 50,000 to 2,000,000 individual spiders, each devouring hundreds of insects per year. The British arachnologist W.S. Bristowe once calculated that spiders in England captured enough insects in a year to exceed the weight of that nation's human inhabitants.

Spiders make frequent appearances in folklore and mythology throughout the world. The ancient Greeks told a myth in which the maiden Arachne engaged in a weaving contest with the goddess Athena. Arachne was the hands-down winner, which so enraged the goddess that she destroyed the girl's creation. Arachne was distraught over this and tried to hang herself, but Athena loosened her noose, changed it to a spider's silk, and transformed Arachne into a spider condemned to weave her tapestries forever. From her name comes Arachnida, the class that includes all spiders, scorpions, harvestmen, ticks, and mites.

Ancient Romans attempted to ward off spiders by carrying agate talismans in their pockets, and Roman soothsayers claimed to see auguries in the patterns in spider webs. Spiders have been considered both lucky and unlucky in many cultures, from the ancient Egyptians, who would place a spider in the home of newlyweds for luck, to much more recent times, when many people have considered it good luck for a new bride to see a spider or walk through a web. In Western traditions, killing a spider (especially at night) has long been considered bad luck. Rural Englanders would throw a spider over their heads and recite: "If you wish to live and thrive, let a spider run alive." If a spider falls on you it means you will soon receive a gift of money. If it scurries across your face you can expect to receive a letter or a visit from a long-lost friend. Step on a spider and you can expect rain within twenty-four hours.

Poor Miss Muffet, who wanted only to eat her curds and whey, was an actual person, the daughter of Thomas Muffet, a physician in sixteenth-century England. The good doctor earned a great deal of notoriety in his time for his faith in prescribing spiders as a cure for almost any ailment or injury. His methods had very old sources. The Greeks wore spiders inside amulets as protection against disease. The Romans believed spiders could cure fever-producing illnesses—a belief given validity in 1882 when the drug arachnidin, isolated from spider webs, was found to reduce fever.

*

Even the most imaginative myths and folklore can hardly match the actual natural history of spiders. If spiders did nothing else, their skill in constructing webs would keep us marveling, though few of us have taken that appreciation to the extreme of Charles Durand, a wealthy Louisiana planter of the nineteenth century. Shortly before the Civil War, Durand celebrated the wedding of his daughter by ordering his servants to collect thousands of spiders and release them in the oak trees that lined the driveway to his mansion. The spiders went to work weaving webs that covered the trees with gossamer. On the morning of the wedding, Mr. Durand illuminated the webs by blowing clouds of gold and silver dust into them with a bellows.

Spiders produce their silk from glands and release it through two to eight appendages on the abdomen known as spinnerets. How they make their webs is a meticulously determined process that varies from species to species, and is innate; even newly hatched spiderlings can weave perfect little webs. When first released the silk is liquid, but it hardens quickly into a material with more tensile strength than steel. Large tropical webs, some measuring eight feet across, are strong enough to trap small birds.

All spiders can produce silk, but not all weave their silk into webs. Wolf spiders, for instance, have no need for webs. With 125 species in North America and fifty in Europe, they are among the most familiar of spiders. Typically about one-half inch to two inches across, and often exhibiting distinctive stripes and other markings, they are fleet-footed ground hunters that capture prey by stalking them and running them down. The ancient Greeks erroneously thought they hunted in packs, so they named them *lykos,* for "wolf." Early taxonomists attached the Latin form, *Lycosa,* to the genus, and the common name stuck. Many species of wolf spiders, including the aptly named trap-door spider, live in burrows they excavate in the ground, from which they rush out to grab insects and other prey as they wander past. Not surprisingly, they are equipped with three rows of eyes that give them exceptional vision. Like all but a few spiders, *Lycosa* bite and inject venom into their prey, immobilizing them and dissolving their insides into a liquid they can ingest at their leisure.

Another family of spiders that hunt by stalking is the Salticidae, or jumping spiders. They are the largest family of spiders, with more than 500 genera and 5,000 species worldwide. Typically rather short-legged and brightly marked, they often leave a silk dragline behind as they jump as far as forty times their own length to escape danger and to pursue prey, sometimes even intercepting insects as they fly past. Their front two legs are often their largest and are used for grasping prey and, in some species, to signal potential mates, but it is the smaller rear legs that pack most of the leaping power. They have the keenest vision of any spiders and are among the most sure-footed, able to quickly climb walls and cross ceilings thanks to tufts of sticky hair known as scopulae on their feet and legs.

Most species of crab spiders—the family Thomisidae—hunt on the prowl or hide among flower blossoms to ambush bees and flies. Many camouflage themselves by selecting flowers that match their body colors. The goldenrod crab spider, *Misumena vatia,* which is found in North America and Europe, takes the strategy a step further by altering its color to match the flower it is hunting on. It appraises color through its eyes, and if the flower is yellow—as it is, for instance, on a goldenrod—the spider secretes yellow pigments into cells on the outer layer of its body. If the flower is white, it excretes the yellow pigments and falls back on its default white color.

Some water-dwelling spiders walk on the surface film of ponds or streams or use their legs as oars. Clinging to a plant stem or other support, they submerge to hunt for aquatic insects, tadpoles, or tiny fish, breathing air from bubbles adhering to their bodies. The only true aquatic spider, *Argyroneta aquatica,* is found in ponds and slow rivers in Europe and Asia. It hunts at night for aquatic insects, and spends its days resting underwater in a dome-shaped silken chamber, in which it stores a bubble of air. When it needs to replenish its oxygen supply it swims to the surface, collects a bubble of air on the hairs of its body, and carries it back to its chamber.

Perhaps the most unusual hunter among spiders is the spitting spider, *Scytodes thoracica*. This small inhabitant of Europe and North America captures prey by stalking them slowly, and, when it is about a third of an inch away, spraying a double stream of sticky venomous silk from the front of its thorax, coating its victims so thoroughly that they have no hope of escaping.

Almost all spiders inject their prey with venom pumped through fangs, a grisly killing technique that is certainly one reason many people are afraid of them. If you do an Internet search on "the most deadly spiders" be prepared to be horrified. Everywhere are lists of the ten most dangerous species, with mortality statistics from around the world and close-up photos of fanged horrors as well as the gruesome wounds they leave on human victims. But the Internet exaggerates. In truth, only a few spiders worldwide are a real risk to humans. In fact, most of the "deadly" spiders turn out to be little threat at all.

Arachnologist Richard S. Vetter has made it his mission to debunk many of the myths that have stuck to spiders like flies in a web. He is an expert on the brown recluse, a North American spider that attracts an abundance of myths and mistruths, and for years has led a campaign to calm the panic that arises from periodic reports of "infestations" of the brown recluse in southern California and elsewhere. In numerous scientific papers and in his book, *The Brown Recluse Spider* (Cornell University Press, 2015), he emphasizes that the recluse, *Loxosceles reclusa,* is found only in the central Midwest, from Nebraska to Texas and as far east as southern Ohio and north-central Georgia. It is a slow moving spider that remains hidden most of the time in dark places such as closets, attics, and basements, and is quite abundant throughout much of its range. Often but not always chocolate brown in color, it is usually marked on the top of its head with a distinctive shape reminiscent of a violin—thus its common names: fiddleback, fiddler, or violin spider. It will bite if squeezed or antagonized, and about ten percent of the bites will develop into necrosis, a rotting of the skin and muscle tissue that sometimes requires skin grafting. Less than one percent of bites cause systemic reactions, usually in children under the age of seven, that can be fatal if not treated.

Vetter reports that the brown recluse was rarely noticed until 1957, when arachnologists determined that its bites occasionally caused skin lesions that were slow to heal. Stories with sensational headlines like "Necrotic Wounds" and "Spider-bite Terror" soon began appearing in the popular press, leading to "outbreaks" of the spider in places where it does not exist. Even where the brown recluse is common, most medical diagnoses of its bites are incorrect and are actually caused by ticks, chiggers, and other biting insects, or are cases of *Streptococcus* bacterial infection, Lyme disease, skin cancer, and other conditions that can be dangerous if not properly identified. As for the spider's alleged spread into California, Vetter could not be more emphatic: "There are no populations of brown recluse spiders living in California. In case this upsets your applecart, I repeat, there are *no populations of brown recluse spiders living in California."*

In its home range the brown recluse is a common house spider that people get along with quite easily. Vetter reports that he and a graduate student once collected forty of them in a barn in Missouri in a little over an hour of searching, and that colleagues found fifty-two of the spiders while cleaning a busy science lab. In Oklahoma, a small group of eighth-grade science students set out to collect insects and in a few minutes, while turning over bricks around their school's flag pole, gathered sixty brown recluses with their bare hands; not one student was bitten. In a period of six months in Kansas a woman collected 2,055 of the spiders in her house; she and her family of four had lived there for eight years without any of them being bitten.

Another common spider myth addressed by Vetter concerns giant deadly spiders from Central and South America hiding in bunches of bananas. Large, scary-looking spiders *do* occasionally stow away in shipments of fruit and other cargo, but the chances of encountering one are slim and they present little risk. The media often identifies the culprit as the armed spider of Brazil, *Phoneutria fera.* This species, also called the Brazilian wandering spider, can be aggressive, is large, with a body length of about two inches and a leg span up to six inches, and is indeed venomous. But it is not nearly as deadly as is often claimed. In a study of 422 people in Brazil that were bitten by three *Phoneutria* species, only about ten required antivenom, and only one, a small child, died. The overwhelming majority of victims reported mild reactions. Is the spider found in bunches of bananas? Probably not. *Phoneutria fera* lives deep in the Amazon rain forest, far from the nearest banana groves. One *Phoneutria* species from the west coast of South America is occasionally transported to North America in the cargo holds of ships, but it is much smaller than other armed spiders and has weak venom.

The majority of spiders that sometimes catch rides in banana shipments are members of the genus *Cupiennius*. One species is often misidentified as *Phoneutria*, even by arachnologists, because, like the potentially dangerous *Phoneutria fera* of the Amazonian interior, it has bright red hairs on its chelicerae (the pair of extended structures on the spider's "face" to which the fangs are attached). But *Cupiennius* are harmless. Scary, perhaps, because they are large and because the stories about deadly spiders lurking inside banana bunches make people jumpy, but their bites are mildly painful at worst.

The black widow spider is probably the most notorious of spiders. The genus, *Latrodectus,* is represented by thirty species worldwide, many of them known as "black widows" although not all of them are dangerous. In Russia their common name translates to "black wolf"; in Croatia as "black hag." In South Africa they're called "black button spiders."

In North America two species of *Latrodectus* are of special concern, the southern black widow (*Latrodectus mactans*) and the western black widow (*L. hesperus*), the females of which can produce venom more potent per drop than that of a rattlesnake. Black, glossy, with a globe-shaped red "hourglass" or other marking on its belly, the black widow bites only under extreme conditions—when handled roughly and squeezed, for instance—and the danger from them is greatly exaggerated. People who live where the southern and western species are most common can usually avoid them by being vigilant in places where the spiders are prevalent, such as in woodpiles and debris piles and in deserted sheds, outhouses, and other structures. The bite leaves two small puncture wounds in the skin, and the venom is a neurotoxin that produces a painful wound that spreads to other parts of the body and can cause severe muscle contractions and flu-like symptoms. During the decade of the 1950s, sixty-three people in the United States were reported to have died of black widow bites. After the development of antivenom and other medical treatment the death-rate fell rapidly. Today fatalities are extremely rare.

Talk about deadly spiders, and many people think of tarantulas. Some giant tarantulas of tropical South and Central America can measure as much as ten inches across when their legs are extended, and they feed on small birds and snakes as well as insects. But American tarantulas rarely bite people and contain a venom too weak to harm large mammals.

In Europe, a wolf spider, *Lycosa tarentula*, has inspired a lively legend. Named for the Italian city of Taranto, this spider is a burrow-dweller thought for centuries to inflict fatal bites on humans. Much of the fear of this virtually harmless species comes from its association with the tarantella—a frenzied, whirling dance purported to result from the spider's venom (conversely, in some legends, the frenzy is said to be *cured* by the tarantula's bite). Some historians have proposed that the association of spider and dance originated as a ruse to get around church edicts that banned dancing, which the church thought was dangerously reminiscent of pre-Christian Dionysian rites. Defiant villagers, determined to kick up their heels, claimed they had been bitten by a *Lycosa* and were merely dancing the effects away.

Spiders have been largely misunderstood when it comes to their danger to humans, but tales of their threats to one another are largely true. Most species are cannibalistic and will feed on smaller or weaker species. Female black widows do not invariably eat their mates, but they and the females of many other species eat them often enough to make mating a hazardous occupation for males. A male spider is usually smaller than the female and is naturally a cautious and jumpy fellow when he has courtship on his mind. He signals his intentions from a distance, plucking at the female's web with a carefully cadenced rhythm or signaling across a reasonable distance by waving his legs in ways he hopes the female will recognize. The male of the nursery web spider, *Pisaura mirabilis*, attempts to satisfy his potential mate's hunger by courting her with a freshly killed and attractively gift-wrapped fly; if she's receptive to his gift, he copulates with her while she is busy eating the insect. The male of the crab spider *Xysticus lanio* woos his mate with caresses. When she is sufficiently relaxed he spins silk around her legs and ties her to the ground so that he can make a clean getaway after mating.

Why are people afraid of spiders? Some of it is pure thrill—we *like* hearing stories about deadly spiders, killer snakes, great white sharks, and man-eating lions and tigers and bears. They give us that delicious shiver up the spine and cause us to draw closer to the campfire.

In the case of spiders, it might simply be their "otherness" that makes our heart race and skin tighten. Those eight legs and bizarre stacked eyes make them seem as alien as creatures from another planet. Psychologists say children learn to fear spiders only because they see their parents and other people react with fear. Some have even suggested that waving our fingers in front of an infant's eyes is menacing to them and teaches them to fear the fingerlike motions of a spider's legs. Still other psychologists think our fear of spiders is instinctive, a case of "prepared learning" that may have its origins in very ancient fight or flight responses. Normally, the sudden increase in heartbeat stimulated by the sight of a spider is followed by the release into the bloodstream of endorphins that act as tranquilizers. One theory is that arachnophobia is caused by little more than the body's failure to release those endorphins.

Any reasonable person knows we have no reason to be afraid. And I, after all, am a reasonable person. I know what can hurt me, and what cannot. Demonstrating to my sons that there is nothing to fear, I bend to look closely at a large, fleet-footed wolf spider we have discovered on the floor of the bathroom. My head says everything's fine, that spiders are fascinating and complex and worthy of close study. We owe a lot to spiders, my head says, and they occupy an important place in the world. I know that, I really do. I repeat it over and over in my head, but all the while my heart is shouting, "Fool! Get away! Don't let it touch you!"

4

PARTY ANIMALS, AND OTHER BEASTLY SYMBOLS

Every election year ballots feature an array of candidates claiming third- and fourth- and sometimes fifth-party allegiance. Rarely do those candidates claim more than a single-digit percentage of the popular vote. While Republican elephants trumpet and Democratic donkeys bray, the Libertarian and Socialist candidates always, so far, slip quietly from view.

An example that many will remember is when billionaire businessman Ross Perot ran for the presidency as an independent in 1992 and 1996. Perot surprised many people by garnering the highest tallies of popular votes by a third-party candidate since Theodore Roosevelt ran as a Progressive in 1912. With his populist, moderate stance on most issues, it appeared for awhile as if Perot might have a chance to win. But in the end, he fell short. Why?

To me the explanation was obvious. Perot's problem from the beginning was that he allied himself with a political party lacking a recognizable animal mascot. He should have lifted an eagle from his celebrated collection of patriotic art, or resurrected Theodore Roosevelt's bull moose. When Perot finally scuttled his 1996 campaign, many wondered if it was because he could not bear the thought of losing. A newspaper pundit proposed that his Reform Party's animal emblem should be a chicken.

I admit it: politics confuses me. My friend Tom Carney, who's no dummy, assures me I'm not alone. He considers the electoral college one of the three most bewildering things in life (the other two are the half-life of isotopes and the fact that his brother-in-law, Jackson, doesn't like cheese). The entire business perplexes me. Why two parties instead of ten? Why any? When my son, Nick, was four years old he constructed a protest sign and carried it around the house for days. The sign read: "I don't understand why Zach's cat runs away from me." I'm tempted to follow the same impulse and make a sign that reads: "I don't understand why elected officials care more about their political parties than they do their nation."

When faced with giant perplexities my inclination is to turn to manageable small ones. On my desk are a pair of Arnold Roth cartoons depicting imaginary meetings of the Republican and Democratic national committees, at which party stalwarts are trying to decide on new animal symbols for themselves. In the first cartoon, the Democrats are at each others' throats and slugging it out over sheets of newsprint scribbled with graffiti and a goofy Pegasus-like horse with wings. In the other, the Republicans are sitting in staid order, their hands raised like bidders at an art auction, while attendants display elegantly framed pictures of chickens, snails, turtles, dinosaurs, a unicorn, and a dodo.

Maybe it's appropriate that the subject of party symbols be addressed in cartoons, since the Republican elephant and Democratic donkey were both invented by the nineteenth-century cartoonist Thomas Nast. In the November 7, 1874, issue of *Harper's Weekly,* a Nast cartoon appeared with an elephant representing the Republican Party being chased by a rabble of other animals. Leading the rabble was a donkey dressed in a lion's skin, representing the anti-Republican *New York Herald*. It's not clear why Nast was inspired to choose those particular animals. His sympathies were obviously Republican, and perhaps he chose an elephant simply because it is such a formidable creature. His donkey was undoubtedly an ass—a symbol for stupidity since ancient times. The lion skin referred to one of Aesop's fables, in which an ass wears a lion's pelt to frighten a fox but gives itself away when it cannot refrain from braying. That the elephant and donkey mascots have survived for so many years is probably due more to Thomas Nast's influence than to the appropriateness of the images. I'm sure the Democrats would like to think so.

In the world of politics and governance, few symbols have been as successful as the bald eagle. It seems obvious to us now, a perfect choice—it announces that we are fierce, brave, independent, and awesomely armed. Yet when the founding fathers set out to select an emblem for our new nation, they did not consider the bald eagle an automatic choice. The July 4, 1776 meeting of the Continental Congress charged Thomas Jefferson, John Adams, and Benjamin Franklin with the task of designing a national seal, but they failed to reach a consensus. So did a second committee in 1780. An offering by Charles Barton in May 1782—a tiny eagle perched above a thirteen-striped shield—was rejected by Congress. Finally, Charles Thomson, secretary of the Congress, came up with an emblem for the national seal—an eagle with a banner reading *E pluribus unum* held in its beak—and on June 20, 1782, the bald eagle officially became our national bird.

Not everyone was pleased. Benjamin Franklin wrote to his daughter to complain that the eagle was a poor choice because it was "a bird of bad moral character... Like those among men who live by sharping and robbing, he is generally poor, and often very lousy. Besides, he is a rank coward." In a passage that is frequently offered as evidence that Franklin advocated the wild turkey as the American symbol, he wrote that compared to the eagle the turkey is "a more respectable bird, and withal a true native original of America....He is, besides, (though a little vain and silly, it is true, but not the worse emblem for that), a bird of courage."

Nobody knows if Franklin was serious in his praise of the turkey, or whether he was indulging in a bit of ornithological whimsy. If he was serious, there was precedent. Old World cartographers had been using turkeys as symbols of the New World since at least 1555, and European silversmiths in the sixteenth and seventeenth centuries frequently used them as embossed emblems representing America, just as they used peacocks for Europe, camels for Asia, and lions for Africa. Even as late as 1826, John James Audubon was promoting the virtues of the wild turkey, making it the first plate in his *Birds of America*. He also engraved its image above the words "America My Country" on the ring he used to seal his documents with wax.

When we think of turkeys these days, many of us think of the notoriously stupid birds bred wholesale in poultry factories. Legends about domestic turkeys drowning during rainstorms because they stared at the sky with their mouths open may have no basis in fact, but we've nonetheless come to use the term "turkey" to mean anything (or anyone) that is foolish, a failure, a dud, a washout, or a fiasco. The notion that wise old Ben Franklin would advocate such a bird to represent the United States is almost irresistible. It was clearly irresistible for the makers of Wild Turkey bourbon, who launched an advertising campaign during the 1970s and 1980s that made liberal use of the Ben Franklin-turkey story, and featured a handsome painting of a wild turkey in flight above the headline, "Part of Our National Heritage."

The success or failure of animal symbols usually depends on the appropriateness of the animal. Eagles are practically failsafe, as Anheuser-Busch and its subsidiary, Eagle Snacks, have discovered. American Airlines once tried to change its logo by eliminating the eagle, but thought better of it when thousands of company employees formed a "Save the Eagle" campaign.

Famous animal mascots seem to be everywhere. In 1947 a black bear in baggy trousers and a ranger's hat pointed a finger at us and said, "Remember, only YOU can prevent forest fires." Suddenly, the world became a safer place. Smokey the Bear, who originated as a cartoon character two years before he accepted his job with the U.S. Forest Service, has appeared on countless posters, print ads, and television commercials, and now enjoys special trademark status bestowed by an act of Congress. In 1950 the National Zoo in Washington, D.C. adopted a black bear cub that had been rescued from a wildfire in the Capitan Mountains of New Mexico. He remained at the zoo as a living Smokey the Bear for twenty-six years and was so popular, and received so much fan mail (as much 13,000 pieces some weeks), that the U.S. Postal Service designated him as his own zip code.

Those of us of a certain age remember Joe, the Arabian dromedary on the cover of Camel cigarette packages, who for many years was one of the most readily recognized mascots in the world. According to Hal Morgan, in *Symbols of America*, R.J. Reynolds Tobacco Company brought out their first packaged cigarette in 1913, made from a blend of Turkish and American tobaccos, and named it Camel in honor of the Turkish ingredient. By coincidence, the Barnum and Bailey circus was in Winston-Salem, North Carolina at the same time graphic designers at R.J. Reynolds were looking for cover art. They sent a photographer to the circus. He snapped a shot of a camel called Old Joe, one of the stars of the troupe, and an artist sketched him in front of a background of palm trees and pyramids. The original art on the cigarette package never changed, but from 1987 to 1997 Old Joe was transformed into a more hip dromedary, complete with a bow tie, Italian suit, and debonair posturing—an image that sparked much controversy and even some lawsuits because it was so appealing to kids that it inspired many to start smoking before they reached legal age.

In 1867, a New York cigar company, Straighton and Storm, was struggling to come up with a catchy name for a new line of cigars. One night (according to company legend), one of the owners, Mr. Storm, was sitting in his Long Island house pondering the problem, when a snowy owl burst through his window. Not one to ignore providence, he named the new line White Owl Cigars, and a snowy owl has appeared as its symbol ever since.

There is hardly a community in America that doesn't support a local chapter of The Benevolent and Protective Order of Elks. Organized in 1868 as a drinking club for vaudeville actors, the Elks have grown to become one of the most successful and secretive of all fraternal organizations. Whatever it is Elks do in their closed-door meetings, it apparently has nothing to do with large ungulates. They chose the name Elks after first rejecting Foxes (because they're "too cunning"), Beavers (because they're "destructive"), and Bears (because they were perceived as "coarse, brutal, and morose").

Animals hold such symbolic importance in the affairs of humans that we sometimes forget how prominent they are. In the financial world, the significance of a bear or bull market is well understood, but the origin of the terms is murky. Some sources say a bear market—one that is in decline, causing a mood of pessimism among investors—originated in a folktale about a man who sold the skin of a bear before he had actually killed the animal (or, in other versions, refers to an old French proverb: "Don't sell the bear's skin before you have killed it"), leading to the expression "bearskin brokers" for those who speculated on stocks they didn't own then sold them in a falling market. A bull market, on the other hand—one that is on the rise, making investors optimistic—may have its origin in the way a bull typically bucks its horns upward while attacking and charges forward with confidence. Others have suggested it was a shortened form of "bully," which originally meant "excellent."

Two familiar symbols that on the surface seem entirely appropriate are hawks for war and doves for peace. Never mind that hawks rarely battle among themselves or that doves and pigeons are among the most quarrelsome of birds. The Roman poet Ovid wrote that hawks are hateful because they "always live in arms," a sentiment shared in early nineteenth-century America by critics of Republican expansionists, or "war hawks." In Genesis a dove returns to Noah with an olive twig to show that the waters of the flood are receding, and in Christian art white doves appear as symbols of the human soul and of the Holy Ghost. When Picasso set out to design a universal symbol of peace he chose, naturally, a dove. During the war in Vietnam, it was an important schoolyard ritual to announce whether you were a hawk or a dove. Like many of my contemporaries, I lacked political backbone and declared myself a hawk early in the war and a dove later. Secretly, I remained a hawk in spirit, having always been fascinated with raptors. Besides, I associated doves with pigeons and was certain it would be more fun to soar on thermal currents than to perch cooing on a statue's whitewashed head.

Some societies have totem animals; we have sports animals. In my home state of Michigan we cheer wildly for the Tigers, Lions, and Redwings with the hope that they will defeat an entire menagerie of Bulls, Bears, Rams, Bucks, Dolphins, Cardinals, Orioles, Seahawks, Black Hawks, Falcons, Eagles, and Penguins. We tend to get extremely patriotic about our animal symbols.

Psychologist Carl Jung believed animal symbols are important to us because we have animal natures as well as spiritual natures. To the Danish mythologist Sven Tito Achen, animals are the most important of all symbols and certainly the most widespread. "From primeval hunting magic," he writes, "to present-day advertising our world is full of the idea that animals are ideal. We would like to be like them. We would like to *be* them!"

Which brings us back to donkeys and elephants. As far as I know, Democrats are not distinguished by their stubbornness and Republicans do not have prodigious memories. If we consider animals so significant in our lives, why do Republicans and Democrats associate themselves with creatures that have no clear connection to their party platforms?

If I could find a politician who would listen to me, this is what I would say: Stop wasting your time and mine bashing opponents and lying to voters, and start reading *Walker's Mammals of the World* and *The Illustrated Encyclopedia of Birds*. You'll find plenty of inspiration in those pages. And you might even pick up a few tips on how to get along with others of your species.

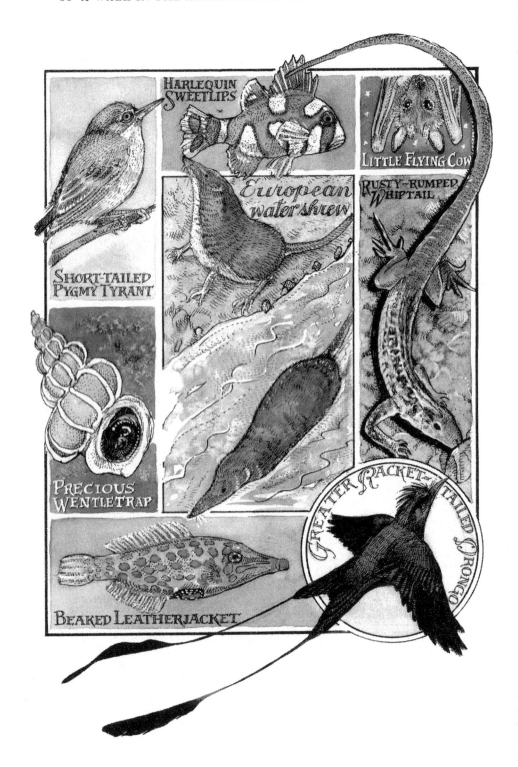

HARLEQUIN
SWEETLIPS

LITTLE FLYING COW

*European
water shrew*

RUSTY-RUMPED
WHIPTAIL

SHORT-TAILED
PYGMY TYRANT

PRECIOUS
WENTLETRAP

BEAKED LEATHERJACKET

GREATER RACKET-TAILED DRONGO

5

THE NAMING OF
THE SHREW

In the beginning was the word, and it's a good thing, because above all else we are creatures of language. Adam's first act was to name the birds of the air and the beasts of the field, and in so defining the things of the world he made it come alive. Little wonder, then, that we are obsessed with giving names to everything we can see and touch and imagine. It's probably our best trick.

Which might explain why, since childhood, one of my favorite rainy-day pastimes has been to browse on animal names. My life list of nomenclature includes some exotics we'll get to, but I keep coming back to the shrew. The word, first of all, is fun to say. Pronounce it slowly, with animation, and you can't help forming the face you might make if you happened to bite into the animal it designates. Many predators avoid shrews because they have glands on their flanks that secrete a nasty-smelling musk that makes them bitter to the tongue. Scrunch up your face and say it: "Shrew!" The word isn't so much spoken as expelled.

Few people observes shrews up close, not because shrews are rare (they're quite common in many places in the world), but because they're small (two to four inches on average), are largely nocturnal, and are almost too shy to live. As you're driving at night you might occasionally see one darting in manic dashes across the road in front of you: a hyperactive bundle of indecision, scampering first one way, then another, then streaking across the pavement so fast you're breathless with sympathy for such a tightly wound package of nerves. If ever a mammal needed to take a breath and relax, this is it.

By any standard, shrews are damned strange animals. Their metabolism operates at full-tilt boogie every moment of their lives, but when they are frightened their hearts can accelerate to a rate of 1,200 beats a minute—about twice that of a hummingbird's heart—and can be halted in mid-beat by sudden loud noises. You could kill that highway dasher with a blast of your car horn.

To maintain their frenetic metabolic, shrews must eat almost constantly, so they can't afford to be choosy. They consume just about anything they find, including earthworms, spiders, centipedes, snails, slugs, insect larvae, lizards, frogs, fish, nuts, seeds, plants, and any mammals and birds small enough or slow enough to be overpowered. Shrews have poor eyesight and hunt seemingly at random, zigzagging across the ground until they blunder into something edible. Some species have a taste for carrion and like to burrow first into the brain of a dead animal. Others, if they can't find anything else to eat, will curl up, lock their hind legs with their forelegs, and snack on their own feces as they defecate.

Some mother shrews and her young travel in caravan, each animal biting the fur on the rump of the one ahead to remain in contact, making them look like a string of furry frankfurters undulating along the ground. If threatened, shrews are likely to rise on their hind legs, bare their teeth, and emit a squeaky warning cry. Like bats, they probably use echolocation to get around in the dark. Some species swim and dive as adroitly as tiny otters; others are equipped with fringes of hair around their feet that allow them to scamper across the surface of ponds and streams. Still others spend most of their lives in trees. One species, the Sichuan burrowing shrew, appears to live almost entirely underground.

Naturally, such odd creatures are magnets for superstition. Shrews for a long time were thought to be so poisonous that they could sicken farm animals just by crossing paths with them. Europeans believed for centuries that the bite of a shrew was venomous, a notion they carried to the New World despite experts' assurances to the contrary. Folklore, said the experts. An old wives' tale. Until some skeptical American biologist picked up a short-tailed shrew and it sank its teeth into his finger, pumped venomous saliva into the wound, and left the biologist a howling believer. It turns out that the northern short-tailed shrew, *Blarina brevicauda*, is the only venomous mammal in North America. Found from southern Saskatchewan to Nova Scotia in the north, and from central Nebraska to central Georgia in the south, it packs poison in its saliva powerful enough to kill a full-grown rabbit, though the ordinary dose is only enough to paralyze a field mouse. The European water shrew also produces venom, with which it subdues fish, frogs, and aquatic larvae while hunting underwater.

In his book *Et Cetera, Et Cetera*, the biologist Lewis Thomas traced the origin of the word *shrew* to its Indo-European root, *skreu*, which served as a verb meaning to cut something up, or as a noun for the tool used in such cutting. Later, in Old English, it became the noun *screawa* and was applied to the animal, perhaps because the shrew can be such a vicious little butcher of prey. In time the word morphed into the Middle English verb "to shrew," which meant simply to curse, inevitably evolving into the adjective "shrewd," meaning "bad, keen, or piercing." A shrew or shrewish person was deceitful and nagging and prone to violent temper tantrums and foul speech, although by the time of the Elizabethans the epithet had softened somewhat. Quick-witted Kate in *The Taming of the Shrew* was an easily recognized character type in Shakespeare's England, feisty and free-spirited, at a time when to be called a shrew could be either a compliment or an insult (thus the audience of *Much Ado About Nothing* knew, as we do today, that to be "shrewd of tongue" was to be spiteful, severe, malicious, and clever). These days nobody likes to be called a shrew, but shrewdness in courtrooms and negotiating sessions earns our grudging admiration.

A word like *shrew* fit its namesake perfectly, but we're not always so practical with our naming. Because we get pleasure from the trill of syllables and the cadence of consonants, we sometimes choose names because they are the audible equivalent of flowers of blossom. Is there a correlation between our words and our notions of beauty? Of course. How else explain the gorgeous names we've bestowed upon butterflies and birds, and the dull ones with which we've burdened bats and reptiles? We'll now and then deign to offer an interesting name to a bat—the little flying cow, for instance, for a small African nectar feeder; and the ghostly white ghost bats of Central and South America; and the African butterfly bats, which resemble moths and butterflies with their spots, stripes, and fluttering flight—but those are the exceptional names in an order that includes a thousand blandly labeled species. Surely it is indicative of our ambivalent attitudes toward bats that the two most common species in North America are called the little brown bat and the big brown bat.

Among reptiles and amphibians, beautiful names are as rare as beautiful faces, but a little digging in the literature uncovers such alliterative gems as the longnose leopard lizard and the savannah slimy salamander. And who can resist the rusty-rumped whiptail? Or the redstripe ribbon snake? Or the bluetail mole skink?

We've given marine animals names that could be characters in a children's book. The notable rattail and southern gobbleguts would make deliciously nasty villains. Ovate silverbiddy and precious wentletrap are surely someone's eccentric maiden aunts. Any kid would be happy to set off on an adventure with the harlequin sweetlips or the bicolor dottyback. Who wouldn't be charmed by a lollipop shark or a rose-petal bubble shell or a honeyhead damsel? Who doesn't feel sympathy for the depressed gorgonian crab?

Most freshwater fish are named less imaginatively than their saltwater cousins, but a few stand out, including the stargazing minnow, virgin spinedace, bluefin stoneroller, warpaint shiner, flannelmouth carpsucker, sharpfin chubsucker, suckermouth redhorse, bigeye jumprock, stippled studfish, rainwater killifish, and frecklebelly madtom.

Of course we've revealed our passion for language most extravagantly with birds. We might not have the opportunity to see every species in the wild, but we can nominally enjoy the fan-tailed berrypicker, tink-tink cisticola, ruddy turnstone, willie wagtail, and white-crested laughing-thrush. Dr. Seuss might have named the greater racket-tailed drongo, the pale-breasted thrush-babbler, and the yellow-rumped tinkerbird. The bearded helmetcrest could be an obscure accessory to medieval armor. The variable seedeater might be a garden tool manufactured by Black and Decker.

Entertaining as those names can be, they carry little weight among scientists, for whom precision usually has to take precedence over poetry. The vernacular creates local color, but it also can create confusion. The shrew that darts through the fields in England is not the same shrew that lives in New Hampshire or Nepal. A biologist needs to know that the American woodcock he studies in Maine is the same bird that elsewhere in North America is called the timberdoodle, bogsucker, woodhen, big eye, midnight rider, whistledoodle, Labrador twister, night partridge, and mudsnipe.

All of which underscores the need for reliable and universal systems of organization. Naturalists since Aristotle have tried to shoehorn plants and animals into a variety of often whimsical classification schemes. One medieval system ranked animals by their level of nobility, with lions and eagles at the top of the heap. Others began with domestic animals and proceeded to wild ones, or from smallest creatures to largest. Early Anglo-Saxon naturalists relied on a system based on modes of locomotion, in which, for example, all snakes, nightcrawlers, intestinal parasites, and dragons were classified as worms, because they were "creeping things." A habitat-based system in the seventeenth century made the beaver kin to the fishes, simply because both lived in water. A remnant of that concept lingered as late as the 1930s, when the muskrat in North America and the capybara in South America were granted papal classification as fishes, allowing Catholics to eat them on Fridays and other days of fasting. That tradition can be seen to this day in the common fishy names we give to aquatic organisms that are clearly not fish: starfish, crayfish, shellfish.

No discussion of animal and plant classifications would be complete without mentioning the whimsical system devised by the Argentine writer, Jorge Luis Borges, in his 1942 story posing as an essay, "The Analytical Language of John Wilkins." In it Borges mentions a taxonomy of animals that he claims he discovered in an old Chinese encyclopedia called *The Celestial Emporium of Benevolent Knowledge*. If you know Borges you know this encyclopedia is (probably) whimsical, was unearthed by a (perhaps) imaginary scholar, and that the list is as much a playful exercise in the agility of words as it is a commentary on our urge to classify the things of the world. According to Borges' Chinese encyclopedia, animals are divided into:

a) those belonging to the emperor
b) those that are embalmed
c) tame or trained ones
d) suckling pigs
e) mermaids and sirens
f) those that are fabulous
g) stray dogs
h) those included in the present classification
i) frenzied ones
j) innumerable ones
k) those drawn with a very fine camelhair brush
l) other ones
m) those that have recently broken a water pitcher
n) those that from a long way off look like flies

Borges' playful list illustrates why a universal classification system was so necessary if we were to increase our knowledge of living things.

The binomial system in use throughout the world today, whereby a pair of Latin or Latinized words designate the genus and species of every living thing, was invented by Swedish botanist Carl Linnaeus (1707-78). Almost immediately it made all previous systems obsolete. Plants had traditionally been grouped into general categories based on characteristics such as size—"shrubs" and "trees," for instance— but Linnaeus brought much-needed precision to the practice by identifying plants according to their sexual characteristics. Class and order were determined by the number of stamens and pistils. Genus described a general structure, such as the anatomy of a fruit or flower. Species referred to easily identified features such as a plant's taste or the shape of its leaves.

Systema Naturae was a vast improvement over previous systems that had sometimes been ridiculously complicated. Before Linnaeus, a butterfly could be burdened with an impossibly unwieldy Latin name such as *Papilio media alis pronis praefertim interioribus maculis oblongis argenteis perbelle depictus.* A contemporary of Linnaeus's, the French scientist Georges Buffon, persisted in grouping animals according to their familiarity, placing horses, donkeys, and cows together, for example, and chickens with pigeons. But Linnaeus's simple and logical system caught on and soon inspired a mania for naming, making it a mark of high honor—and a source of intense competition—to name a species after oneself or an acquaintance. Linnaeus himself honored a former teacher, Professor Olof Rudbeck, by granting the name Rudbeckia to the genus of flowers we know as coneflowers and black-eyed susans.

Because of Linnaeus the American woodcock became *Scolopax minor* and the greater North American short-tailed shrew became *Blarina brevicauda.* The ancient Greek botanist Isodorus would have been pleased. It was he who said, "If you do not know the names, the knowledge of things is wasted."

Linnaeus lived to see his system revolutionize taxonomy and to allow scientists throughout the world to communicate about the vast numbers of new plants and animals they were discovering in the New World and elsewhere. The first edition of *Systema naturae*, published in 1735, listed about 4,000 species of plants and animals. The tenth edition, in 1758, raised the number to 9,000. By the end of the nineteenth century, biologists had named more than 500,000 living things. Today the total exceeds 1.75 million. Scientists estimate that another six or seven million organisms have not yet been named.

Walt Whitman, who had little interest in classification and taxonomy, wrote in his sprawling memoir of nature-watching, *Specimen Days and Collect*, "You must not know too much, or be too precise or scientific about birds and trees and flowers and water-craft; a certain free margin, and even vagueness… helps your enjoyment of these things." Whitman worried that words might get in the way of a pure appreciation of nature.

But words can be appreciated for their own sake as well. Without our passion for them, the sky would be crossed only by little gray birds and big black birds. We would admit little difference between an elk and a moose, between a skink and a snake, between trout and bullhead and bass. A beaver would be a rat would be a mouse would be a shrew. Which would be a shame, because a shrew is certainly not a mouse, and our lives are much enriched by the difference.

6
CRY COYOTE

Sometimes nature comes pounding at your door, whether you're ready or not. One winter night, my wife, sons, and I put our ski jackets on over our bathrobes, tucked our pajama legs into our boots, and went outside to the field to watch a remarkable trilogy of astronomical events. Comet Hale-Bopp hung low in the sky, beaming like a motorcycle headlight in fog. High above us, Mars glowed bright and faintly red in unusual conjunction with the moon. The moon itself was in eclipse, its light dimming gradually, nibbled away by the Earth's curved shadow. As the moonlight faded, the comet brightened and the snow covering the field and the hills beyond glowed with an eerie, copper-tinted light. We watched until everyone grew cold, then ran shouting in exhilaration back to the house.

A few days later, Nick and I were standing in front of the big window in our living room when a coyote came trotting down our driveway and crossed the yard twenty feet from us. It was a big moment for Nick. He had never seen a coyote in the wild and none of our family or neighbors had ever seen one on the twenty-mile-long peninsula where we live. It is land checkered with woodlots, cherry orchards, vineyards, and subdivisions, a fine mix of habitats well suited for coyotes. But the peninsula is separated from the mainland by five miles of Lake Michigan on each side and is cut off at its base by our small city.

I was so surprised by the animal before us that I barked "Coyote!" It heard me through the glass and instantly turned and ran in a fluid lope across the yard and into the field where we had watched the comet and eclipse. The coyote was a healthy and well-fed specimen, its lush winter coat the color of granite, with highlights of silver, brown, and black—the subtle shades of tree trunks and leafy ground and fallow fields. I knew it wouldn't be long before the varmint hunters mobilized.

The odd thing about varmint hunters in our neighborhood is that some of them are cherry farmers and vineyardists who face perennial trouble from rodents. When meadow voles and field mice become unusually abundant, as they do every few years, they can not find enough food during the winter so they feed on the bark of cherry trees and grape vines. The trees and vines are much affronted by this and die. Dead plants don't produce fruit, so the farmers lose money. Some of the farmers sense profound ecological principles at work but seem to be confused about cause and effect. Instead of welcoming the predators that feed on bark-eating mice and voles, they set out to shoot or trap them. They're especially tough on red fox, and deeply suspicious of hawks and owls. There's not much chance that coyotes will ever be welcome here.

Sure enough, a week after Nick and I saw the coyote in our yard, the local newspaper printed a letter to the editor written by a man who had watched three coyotes emerge from the woods beside his house on our peninsula and give chase to his Scotch terrier. Fortunately, the terrier made it safely to the house, but the man felt it was his duty to sound the alarm. Something had to be done, he cried.

My neighbors divided quickly into opposing camps. One camp included those who are charmed by the idea that a bit more wildness has returned to our over-civilized peninsula. To them the coyotes overcame great odds to arrive here (probably crossing the ice over Grand Traverse Bay that winter), filling an ecological niche and thriving where no coyotes have thrived for many years. Their group includes anti-hunters and suburban nature romantics, as well as hunters (and I am one of them) who have studied enough wildlife biology to know that killing top-tier predators has deleterious consequences throughout an ecosystem.

The other camp was made up of those who persist in considering coyote, wolf, and even eagles and hawks as worthless at best and dangerous at worst. They take for granted that predators kill deer, elk, moose, grouse, pheasant, and other game animals, as well as domestic chickens, sheep, and cattle. To those folks, predators are competition, and not to be abided.

It's an ancient attitude, of course, probably as old as humanity itself, and one that has significantly shaped our attitudes and policies regarding coyotes. In 1915, the U.S. federal government initiated the first large-scale program of coyote control. "Control," of course, meant trapping, poisoning, and shooting hundreds of thousands of adult coyotes, on the ground and from airplanes, as well as killing coyote pups in their dens. Few animals have endured such relentless persecution.

But by the 1960s biologists had concluded that predation by coyotes was not as severe a problem as western ranchers claimed, and that coyotes preyed primarily on the mice, voles, hares, and other small herbivores that those same ranchers had been trying very hard to eradicate because they competed with cattle and sheep for grass. By then it was also evident that the favored coyote controls of traps and poisons were indiscriminately destroying foxes, badgers, cougars, bobcats, lynx, eagles, hawks, and domestic dogs. To top it off, the control measures weren't even very successful. When ranchers began lacing carcasses of cows with strychnine, wolves and other animals died by the thousands, but coyotes avoided the lethal bait.

In 1972 the federal government banned the use of poisons on federal land and in federal predator-control programs, but a black market in banned poisons thrived. Two years later, the estimated kill of coyotes in seventeen western states surpassed 300,000 animals. Not even the wily coyote could withstand such pressure. It virtually disappeared from central Texas, much of North Dakota, and from sheep-grazing country in parts of Colorado, Wyoming, Nevada, and Utah.

Throughout the American West many ranchers and farmers still shoot coyotes on sight. Yet, in most of the western states, coyote numbers are holding steady, and in many other parts of the country they are increasing. Thousands of them live in Los Angeles and in suburban Chicago, Houston, Kansas City, and Brooklyn. Within the past hundred years, the coyote has expanded its range across the United States to the eastern seaboard, north across Canada and Alaska, and south as far as Central America. It might be the ultimate triumphant underdog.

Many people are ambivalent about this, just as they're ambivalent about nature in general. We can go weeks or months without being aware of the wild outside our doors, then it makes an appearance and ancient reflexes are stirred. The fables, myths, folktales, legends, and fairy tales of people everywhere suggest just how deeply are lives are interwoven with the creatures we share the planet with and how complex are feelings are about them.

Many psychologists are convinced that hearing, reading, and telling animal stories in an important step in teaching children to orient themselves in the world. Such stories seem designed to remind us that there are both similarities and differences between people and animals. Fables, nursery rhymes, and fairy tales identify and stereotype behavior in animals—the gluttony of a pig, the cunning of a fox—behavior that children learn also to recognize in themselves and in adults. When a kid plays the role of a grumpy bear or a courageous lion, the animal is serving as a model that helps the child understand grumpiness and courage. It creates a widely shared reality—everybody knows a lion is courageous—that helps the child learn what courage feels like.

When we accuse someone of being a wolf, a bear, or a chicken we perpetuate characterizations that go back hundreds and often thousands of years. The early Greek fables were among the first we know of that associated recognizable character traits with animals and applied them to human situations. Later, the Medieval bestiaries performed a similar task by attributing Christian values to animal behavior. Throughout the world there is an enormous warehouse of myths and tales, many of which share similar motifs. If you want to know how humans feel about animals, that warehouse is a good place to look.

Coyotes show up frequently in the mythology and oral traditions of Native Americans throughout the western United States and Mexico, in what was the historical range of wild coyotes. In many of the oldest traditions, Coyote is featured as a trickster and buffoon. He is not an animal, but one of the First People, a race of godlike mythical beings that lived on Earth before humans came along. They were the creators of the world, the builders of cultures, and the progenitors of the first human beings. It wasn't until after humans appeared that the First People were transformed into animals.

The tales of Coyote the Trickster describe a creature that can change into human form at will, thus linking animals to humans and nature to culture. Like other Tricksters—familiar examples are Reynard the Fox in thirteenth-century France, and Bugs Bunny and Wile E. Coyote in twentieth-century America—he's an altogether lovable scoundrel. He is thieving, deceitful, cunning, crafty, vain, larcenous, and lecherous. He has tremendous vitality. Because of his pranks, rivers now flow only downstream instead of both ways, and people must walk uphill as well as downhill. Because he meddled with the Earthmaker's original creation, where food was always at hand and everyone lived forever, there is death in the world. In the various trickster tales, Coyote suffers many misadventures, including poisoning, starvation, dismemberment, falling, burning, drowning, and annihilation by explosion, but he always bounds back to his robust self. He's outrageous and selfish and bad, and he spends most of his time getting into mischief. Yet he is capable of generous deeds. He taught tribes along the Columbia River how to catch salmon. He stole fire from the gods and carried it as a flame on the tip of his tail and presented is as a gift to people.

Old Man Coyote shares a number of qualities with the biological coyote, which zoologists say is perhaps the most ancient canid in North

America. Fossil remains of primitive coyotes date back four to ten million years, to the late Miocene and early Pliocene. The coyote we know, *Canis latrans*, has lived here for about 500,000 years and for most of that time shared the continent with the mastodon, camel, dire wolf, and sabertooth cat.

Like the Coyote of mythology, the biological coyote is a thief, a wanderer, and a clown. Biologists and storytellers agree that he seems indestructible. He's a work-in-progress—still changing, a master of adaptation. According to an old saying in the American West, "A coyote will eat anything that doesn't eat him first." If there is no game to eat, he eats carrion; if there is no carrion, he eats grasshoppers, fruits, and berries. He's a troublemaker and an escape artist. He pokes around where he has no business. He breeds with wolves and domestic dogs, spawning hybrids that are bigger, stronger, and even more adaptable.

Here on Old Mission Peninsula coyotes are being blamed for everything from plundered garbage cans to the scarcity of certain songbirds. Farmers suspect them of stealing their chickens and rooting up their gardens. When his cat came home with a deeply lacerated front paw, my neighbor was convinced that it was the work of coyotes. At the grocery store I saw a small cluster of people reading a notice on the community bulletin board—"Lost: Yellow Lab, male, four months old"—and heard one of them cluck in regret and whisper, "Coyotes."

The comet has disappeared now, but the Trickster remains. It's funny that we need centuries to change the way we think, but require almost no time at all for coyote to become Coyote.

7
TWO LANES,
NO SHOULDERS

"Improvement makes straight roads; but the crooked roads without
improvement are roads of Genius."
—William Blake, "Proverbs from Hell"

We're fortunate in northern Michigan to do much of our traveling on country roads, and fortunate also that our early road-makers rarely had the luxury of plotting the shortest route between two points. Usually they had no choice but to follow the contours of the land, seeking valleys and plateaus and avoiding swamps, gullies, and lakes. If many of our roads have the circuitous appearance of game trails, it's probably because they began that way. On the best of them, even at sixty miles per hour with the windows closed and the radio on, it's possible to feel yourself wandering rather than hurtling across the land. Go slower, with the windows open, and you seem to meander an older, slower age.

I grew up near what we always describe as the little finger of Michigan. In this part of the Mitten—as across most of Michigan—there's so much water that the land is shaped and defined by it, producing many peninsulas, oxbows, marshes, and bogs, and inspiring almost as many Harbor Views, Bay Views, River View Estates, and Chateau Baysides. The roads here were not built geometrically, as they were across the flatlands of the Midwest, where section-line roads were laid in precise square-mile grids, oriented north-south and east-west, as straight as draftsmen's tools could make them. To build roads in northern Michigan road-makers had to be pragmatic. They could rarely indulge in right angles, could never expect to see a byway run true to a perspective point on the horizon. Their roads snaked, cut back, looped around, and roller-coasted, like lines of poetry rather than lines of Euclid. When we were kids, my brother and our friends and I traveled them standing behind the cabs of our fathers' pickups, gripping the rain gutters, leaning into the hills, bracing our thighs against the curves. We learned the shapes of roads in our muscle memory.

When we traveled on bicycle, as we did every day the weather allowed, pedaling to a friend's house or to the old country store at the north end of the lake, it was always an expedition. Even if we were going only a mile or two we went prepared for emergencies. In fact, of course, we were hoping for them. We carried matches and pocketknives, clipped canteens to our belts, drew cunningly detailed maps. You never knew when you might be caught in a blizzard or get jumped by gangs of lunatics escaped from the State Hospital in Traverse City or be attacked by Soviet invaders sneaking down from the Arctic. We were thrilled to believe that wilderness lurked nearby with all its dark perils. Wolves and coyotes, black bears and cougars lay in ambush in every woodlot and swamp. We would race past the old lilac thicket we had passed every day for years—cresting the same hill, skirting the same line of cedars—and it was always as if we were seeing it for the first time. The setting changed with every curve and hill, so we could never see where we were going or where we had been, only where we were. There was virtue in that. The curves and hills in abundance and the irrational intersections kept us more alert to the world.

For a road to qualify as a country road it must be gravel or roughly paved, and relatively narrow. Six paces from edge to edge is about right, although less is better because it forces opposing automobiles to slow. If there must be a centerline, let it be so old that the yellow paint has settled into the asphalt, giving it the patina of a 1933 license plate nailed to the wall of a barn. Such a road might nudge nature aside, but it can't stop it from crowding the shoulders. You step off and are instantly to your knees in meadow grasses and milkweeds or are immersed in the cool shade of road maples. A shrew bursts blindly into the open, finds itself exposed on the pavement, and dashes across to the safety of the weeds on the other side. If the road were to be abandoned, roots would soon hoist and buckle the pavement and seedlings would pry through every crack. In a few years it would be as overwhelmed as a Mayan temple in a rainforest.

One of the advantages of country roads is that they can accommodate traffic other than cars and trucks. Pedestrians, horses, wagons, bicycles, and tractors are equally welcome. Take a walk with your dog and you'll end up smiling at folks on horseback, nodding at joggers, striking up conversations with interesting people of all sorts. Someone stops beside you on her bike and asks if this is the road to Mapleton. Nice looking dog, she says, what breed? A farmer on a tractor slows and nods his head a half inch in greeting and doesn't accelerate again until he's far enough past to avoid offending you with his exhaust cloud. People in cars make eye contact and often wave. Because you can't always see the driver through the windshield glare, you get in the habit of waving at everyone.

The names of country roads often reveal a kind of unconscious poetry. My wife and I often drive slowly along Seven Hills Road to count the hills and return home on Smoky Hollow Road to see if it is smoky down in the hollow (it is, on winter evenings when smoke from woodstoves is pressed to the ground by atmospheric inversion).

One road we visit regularly winds through a taut and narrow valley of hardwoods to a bluff at the edge of Lake Michigan. It follows the route water took when it poured from the face of glaciers; now it's a lazy ramble through the woods, a winding trail, a glissade.

Another passes beneath a thick canopy of maples that were planted in a flawless row in 1876, in commemoration of the nation's centenary. Where the maples end is a vista of of orchards laid chock-a-block on the hillsides, with an unexpected and stunning view of the big lake beyond. Everywhere the land shows evidence of glacial work. Where the hills and fields are fallow, you can see the bones of the planet beneath them.

Even well-traveled roads can be fruitful places to see wildlife. Like rivers, they form edge habitats that attract specific communities of plants and animals that thrive in such transition zones. Many of those zones can support up to three times the diversity of a hardwood forest or a sedge meadow.

Raptors find the open space along a road productive for hunting, while migrating birds of all kinds may follow north-south roads because they are such convenient and reliable landmarks. At twilight in spring and fall you can sometimes see solitary woodcock fluttering above the road, then flaring off into stands of aspen to feed and rest. Pheasants and other gallinaceous birds go to roads and their shoulders to seek gravel, which their gizzards require to aid digestion. Songbirds take dust baths in the sand along the shoulders and drink from puddles in gravel roads. Vultures, crows, and many other scavengers feed on roadkill.

Going to the road is often, of course, a terrible mistake. Modern roads are such recent phenomena—it's astonishing to remember that in 1902 there were just eighteen miles of asphalt road in the United States—that animals have not had time to adapt to their dangers. On cool nights so many snakes seek the lingering warmth of pavement that in many areas local populations have been annihilated. In spring, when frogs and toads emerge from hibernation and move en masse to ponds for breeding, they are often forced to cross deadly roads along the way. Animals that are nocturnal or crepuscular are most at risk, because they are difficult for motorists to see and because their light-sensitive eyes cause them to be mesmerized and blinded by oncoming headlights. That is why skunks, raccoons, opossums, armadillos, and white-tailed deer make up a disproportionate percentage of animals killed by automobiles.

Roads are such dangerous places for animals that along many of them the most frequently seen wildlife is roadkill, or "road fauna," as biologist Roger Knutson prefers it. Knutson is one of North America's leading experts on road-killed wildlife. His field guide, *Flattened Fauna*, was a surprise bestseller and inspired a generation of flattened-fauna fanatics, including a cadre of enthusiasts who found voice for a time in *Roadkill Quarterly*, an on-line magazine out of Nova Scotia that celebrated the diversity of road-flattened critters and disseminated a seemingly endless stream of "thump-thump" jokes.

Despite Knutson's whimsical tone in *Flattened Fauna* (it is about animals, he writes, that "are not just merely dead but really most sincerely dead"), the book reveals careful research and is a useful identification guide. The silhouette illustrations, some of them produced by scraping animals off roads and placing them on the glass of a photocopier, are helpful in identifying specimens as you speed past at fifty-five miles per hour. Knutson notes that the density of road fauna along most highways varies from .429 to 4.10 animals per mile, and that if you drive from Boston to Chicago you can expect to count from 400 to 3,000 flattened animals.

He also notes that people see from five to twenty-five animals dead on the road for every one they see alive. Enthusiasts sometimes keep "death lists." One such list detailed nine reptiles, fifty-eight birds, and 161 mammals during a 500-mile trip. A world's record may have been set in 1933, when 598 dead rabbits were counted along fifty miles of road near Boise, Idaho.

But all is not morbid in the annals of road-kill biology. Much useful information can be gleaned from the flattened animals on our roads and shoulders, including data about migration and population dynamics. A wildlife biologist in Michigan recently said in an interview that the best way he and his colleagues knew to keep track of the population cycles of "little stuff"—opossums, raccoons, squirrels, ground hogs, and porcupines—was to note how frequently they were seen as roadkill. The opossum population was down in northern Michigan, he said, perhaps as a result of recent harsh winters. And because opossums prey on birds' eggs, we could probably expect to see an increase in the numbers of grouse, woodcock, turkey, waterfowl, and other ground-nesting birds.

Unlike the enthusiastic correspondents that kept *Roadkill Quarterly* viable, most of us are probably more interested in living animals. We might remember none of the flattened fauna we've seen but probably have vivid memories of living ones. My own memories form a kind of scrapbook from a lifetime of road trips. The great horned owl that swooped through my headlights on a back road in Michigan, a hare hanging limp in its talons. The snowy owl that appeared suddenly, another night, flaring against the side window, its flash of white wings so broad and bright that the three of us inside the car threw up our arms to protect ourselves. The enormous black bear that raised its head and looked at me over a small hill in northern Ontario at the moment I passed in my car. The pair of bull elk Tom Carney and I watched sparring beside the road near his cabin. American kestrels so evenly spaced on telephone wires in North Dakota that they looked like sentries on a parapet.

Years ago, as my family and I were driving across Newfoundland, my oldest son, Aaron, who was eleven at the time, suddenly shouted, "Stop! There's a moose!"

I had doubts. Not because moose are rare in Newfoundland—in fact, they're a formidable traffic hazard—but because already that trip Aaron had sounded several false alarms. We were in highland woods, the road cutting through thickets of willow so dense it was hard to imagine a large mammal could make its way through them. But I stopped the truck and backed up anyway. And there, etched in a wall of twigs and branches, were the antlers and snout and finally the shoulders and spindly legs of a bull moose. We watched until it took a step backward into the willows and disappeared. Then we continued down the road.

Ten minutes later Nick, who at three years old was determined to be his older brother's equal in every way, yelled, "Stop! A monkey!"

Because the world is full of surprises, and because Nick wanted so badly to see a monkey, I braked to a stop and backed up. We scanned the woods carefully, but saw nothing. "He must have run away," I said, and Nick agreed. We drove on, our senses so alert to wonders that Newfoundland still seems a place of magical possibilities, and the miles flew beneath our wheels.

8
WILD PETS

We're a family of animal lovers, but Nick loves them most of all. When he was a toddler he would walk up fearlessly to any dog and try to kiss it and would snag any passing cat and pull it into a crushing hug. At age three he tried for months to capture small mammals, first by leaving bits of cheese near the doors to lure them inside, then by fashioning elaborate traps in the kitchen and living room. We grew accustomed to stepping over boxes held up with popsicle sticks, and over ropes stretched between chairs to which were attached dangling spatulas, eggbeaters, rubber bands, paperclips, and small baskets filled with tiny cubes of cheese. Nick had his heart set on making pets of mice, squirrels, and hares—not to mention porcupines, skunks, and bobcats—and was nearly heartbroken when he failed to introduce any wild animals into his menagerie.

It was an impulse I remembered well from my own childhood. In an aquarium in my bedroom I maintained a rotating population of turtles, frogs, toads, and snakes, most of which died of mysterious ailments or somehow escaped while I was at school, and was always on the lookout for new additions. One day my father came home from work with a tiny raccoon he had found along the highway beside its dead mother. The poor thing was wide-eyed and trembling, as tiny as a kitten, and helpless. It did not stay helpless for long.

For a few days my brother Rick and I took turns cradling it belly up in our arms and feeding it warm milk from a baby bottle. Then it turned into a pet from hell. It loved to run at full speed around the perimeter of the living room, leaping across the tops of the couch and easy chair and onto any handy human's shoulder, where it would hang on for all it was worth with needlelike claws. If you waved a white rag or a handkerchief or one of my father's white shirts, it would attack from hiding and launch itself through the air like the devil's own hunting leopard.

We managed to keep it for about a month, during which it destroyed the upholstery on the couch and chairs, shredded shirts and trousers and socks, got into the cupboard and tore open bags of flour and dried peas, and inflicted flaming scratches across Rick's and my arms and legs. Dad finally donated the little terrorist to the local zoo, where it promptly made enemies with all the other raccoons and had to be placed in solitary confinement. It grew to be very fat and enjoyed a long and notably irascible life there.

Not long afterward, when I was about twelve years old, I was riding my bicycle along the road a few miles from home and spotted a white-tailed deer standing in the ditch. I braked, got off my bike, and stood beside it, breathless, afraid to move. I could hardly believe my eyes. The deer stood in the ditch only twenty or thirty feet away, watching me. I expected at any moment that it would leap away into the woods, as every other deer I had ever seen had done. When it remained there, apparently unafraid, I felt a kind of charm settle around me. It was an old fantasy brought to life: that we are friends with the animals.

Then the deer walked toward me. It came forward without hesitation, right up to me, and pushed its snout beneath my hand like a dog demanding to be petted, forcing my hand to the top of its head. I petted it. I worked my fingers through the coarse hair on its skull to the warm skin beneath and rubbed the scalp between the ears. Two acorn-sized nubs pressed against my fingers. Like I, it was a young buck.

My heart pounded. I was old enough to know that the natural world is not a Disney concoction, that wildlife live in a swirling interplay of hunters and hunted, with predators that kill without pity and prey that die without expecting it. But petting that deer made me feel part of the sentimental world of books and movies I had grown up with, the boy-and-his-wolf and girl-and-her-grizzly romances that we love because they portray the world as a benign and compassionate place filled with creatures that befriend us and protect us from bullies, kidnappers, poachers, and unethical land developers. For those few minutes along the road I believed that the world was benevolent and that kindness and trust were natural laws as inviolable as birth and death. The deer pressed its head into my lap, like a unicorn into the lap of a maiden. I caressed it. I put my arms around it and hugged it. And it responded. It wanted my affection. I think it could have fallen asleep in my arms. Finally I tried to pull away, but the deer pressed insistently against me. I maneuvered my bike between us and started to ride away, but it ran beside me, bleating. In the end I had to peddle as fast as I could to get away.

When I got home and told my parents what had happened and how it had felt to embrace a wild deer, they broke the news to me that it was not a wild deer at all. A neighbor had told them about the deer. It had been adopted as a fawn and raised by a family who lived in the house across the road from where I had encountered it. Its mother had been killed by a car, and the people had taken it home, fed it from a bottle, and raised it until it was weaned. But it had become a pest. It was lonely and wanted constant attention and had learned to ring the doorbell with its nose and wake the family at three and four o'clock every morning. They tried taping over the button, but the deer just stood outside their door and bleated pitiably, like a heartbroken lamb, and kept them awake all night. They led the deer as far into the woods across the road as they could manage, then ran home. It followed them. Eventually they loaded it into the back of a pickup and drove it far out into the national forest and released it.

Of course acts of kindness don't always end well. A deer unafraid of humans is ill-equipped for survival. A black bear accustomed to handouts of human food can starve when forced to return to a diet of berries and grubs. But the urge to protect, possess, and tame wild animals is ancient and perhaps irresistible. It explains how wolves became malamutes and wild cats became tabbies. We want to reach out to nature and touch some tangible part of it and in the process bring a bit of wildness into our lives. Surely it's why we build zoos, aviaries, and aquariums. Just as surely it is why tales of wildlife raised by humans—and humans raised by wildlife—are among the most enduring of stories.

Our ancient tendency to exert dominion over the fish of the sea and the fowl of the air is often ugly and destructive, but it can also reveal our better nature. Many places have laws against keeping wildlife as pets—even, technically, against caring for the injured and orphaned—forcing many people into acts of civil disobedience. Tending an injured starling or nursing a foundling raccoon with a bottle are wonderful ways to gain insights into the lives of creatures we might otherwise know only from a distance.

One winter day when Nick was five years old a meadow vole wandered into our house. We placed it in a hamster cage and fed it sunflower seeds and peanut butter. Nick named it Mike (for its genus, *Microtus*), and watched hour after hour, enchanted, as it nosed around the edges of the cage and nibbled at seeds. It seemed like a sweet-tempered little guy, much more tranquil than any rodents we had known. But after a few weeks, it weakened and died. Nick was devastated.

We tried to convince him that wild animals rarely make good pets and don't adapt well to domestication. We explained that birds need to fly and frogs need to jump and that his wild animal friends were better off having their freedom. It took time for him to get used to the idea but in the end he chose to release most of his animals back into the wild, and we were all a little wiser for the experience.

9
SHAKESPEARE'S BIRDS

We meddle. Apparently we can't resist. Consider Eugene Schieffelin, the amiable drug manufacturer who in the 1890s allegedly tried to bring all the birds mentioned by Shakespeare to North America. Although questions remain about his motives and the degree of his involvement, there's no doubt that Schieffelin captured some birds and carried them across the Atlantic to the United States. After all, as a member of the American Acclimatization Society, it was his *duty*. The Society's mission was to introduce to North America "such foreign varieties of the animal and vegetable kingdom as may be useful or interesting." These days, of course, we realize what a bad idea that was. It should surprise no one that the American Acclimatization Society went extinct long ago.

Schieffelin is sometimes blamed for bringing the English sparrow across the Atlantic—where Americans eventually began calling it the house sparrow—but if he did, he wasn't the first. According to Ted R. Anderson's exhaustively researched natural history, *Biology of the Ubiquitous House Sparrow*, this sparrow, the most widely distributed bird in the world, was first introduced to North America in 1850, when eight pairs were carried to Brooklyn by the staff of the Brooklyn Institute (which later became the Brooklyn Museum). In 1852 or 1853, another 100 individuals were brought on a steamship from Liverpool to New York City and released. Subsequent releases in New York, Philadelphia, Ohio, Michigan, and Wisconsin ensured their survival on this side of the Atlantic.

Schieffelin might not have brought sparrows to the New World, but the evidence is pretty clear that he brought skylarks, nightingales, chaffinches, song thrushes, and bullfinches, none of which survived. Donald Peattie, in his 1941 memoir *The Road of a Naturalist*, suggests that Schieffelin might have tried to transplant European robins, thrushes, and blackbirds as well, again without success. Then in 1890 and 1891 Eugene carried cages full of starlings across the Atlantic—40, 60, 80, or 100 of them, depending on the sources—and released them into New York's Central Park. America's sky would never be the same.

Nor would America's cities, forests, or fields. Within a few decades, starlings in flocks of thousands—and sometimes millions—descended on farmers' fields and orchards and devoured crops by the tons. They devoured insects, as well, but most agronomists agree that the birds have been far more harmful than beneficial. The U.S. Department of Agriculture estimated in 2014 that starlings cost farmers about a billion dollars a year. They're bullies, also, shoving aside bluebirds, woodpeckers, and other native birds that nest in holes and claiming those nesting sites for themselves. And because starlings roost and feed in such enormous flocks, their droppings spread diseases such as toxoplasmosis, a lung disease spread by Toxoplasma parasites; histoplasmosis, an infection caused by breathing in the spores of a fungus found in bird droppings; and Newcastle disease, which is fatal to chickens and other poultry as well as wild birds.

Starlings have been an airborne hazard, as well, in part because they flock in large numbers and because they are individually much denser in body mass than most other birds. In 1960 a flock of an estimated 20,000 starlings flew into the path of a propeller-driven Lockheed Electra shortly after it took off from Boston's Logan Airport, stalling its engines and causing the plane to crash into Boston Harbor, killing sixty-two of the seventy-two passengers and crew on board. It remains the deadliest bird strike in the history of U.S. aviation.

It took a few years for the birds to thrive after Schieffelin released the first of them in Central Park in 1890 and 1891. Soon after, a pair was found nesting in the eaves of the Museum of Natural History near the park, an event noted with interest by a few observant New Yorkers. Half a dozen years later the birds had strayed beyond Manhattan and were soon nesting as far south as Florida and as far north as Alaska. They ate just about anything, and they reproduced prodigiously.

Students of invasive species will recognize the pattern. An animal or plant finds a new ecosystem to its liking, with few natural predators, and suddenly its population explodes and the invader begins destroying habitat and decimating endemic species. Often a domino effect results. Rats escape from ships to Pacific islands and destroy crops and stored food. Farmers import mongoose and release them to prey on the rats, but instead they prey on easier-to-catch reptiles, amphibians, and ground-nesting birds, resulting in decimation and often extinction of them. The list of such invasions is long. Burmese pythons in the Everglades. Rabbits and cane toads in Australia. Kudzu vine and fire ants in the American South. Sea lamprey and zebra mussel in North America's Great Lakes. Wherever we introduce non-native species, ecosystems must absorb the shock. And the shock is often great. Cornell University ecologists have tallied more than 30,000 non-indigenous plant and animal species that have been introduced into the United States. The cost to the nation is estimated at more than $125 billion per year.

The starling infestation is interesting because it became so widespread so quickly and because we can document the changes in public sentiment as the bird established itself. A search through the archives of *The New York Times* uncovers a chronicle of evolving opinion as the birds spread across North America. On March 2, 1900, in a letter to the editors, a city resident named E. Brown asked:

Can you inform me what sort of bird it is which frequents this neighborhood, answering closely the description of a starling, viz., brown plumage, penciled, and darker on head than body; beak about one inch long, and rich yellow color; tail rather short, and legs rather long? ... It may be found almost any clear morning on a large tree in a yard at the southwest corner of Seventy-fifth Street and the Boulevard. Do you know of any foreign birds having been liberated in this city besides sparrows, and by whom? Research has so far failed to identify these birds.

The editors responded:

In reply to the above questions, William T. Davis, a Staten Island naturalist, who is familiar with the birds in this vicinity, says: "There seems to me to be no doubt that Mr. Brown has been observing the starling...A flock of about forty starlings was liberated by Mr. Eugene Schieffelin in Central Park in March, 1890. A pair of these birds built their nest in the roof of the Natural History Museum, at Seventy-seventh Street, in May, 1892, and another pair were seen with their young on the lawn of a residence on Riverside Drive during the same year. At that time their fate as resident birds was far from certain, but now there are colonies in many places near the city. Many starlings may be seen at times in the tall trees at Livingston, S.I. They have also been observed in Prospect Park, Flatbush, Spuyten Duyvil, New Rochelle, Oyster Bay, and Pelham Bay Park."

Davis proceeded to bestow praise that was probably shared by most people, at first:

They are common in England and over most of Europe, and, as they devour insects, they are of use to the farmer. It is said that they will eat potato bugs. Their nests are usually built in the eaves of buildings and in old hollow trees, and their whistling is pleasant and cheerful. As the starling has not been found to interfere with other birds, we may be glad that he has come to stay.

A decade and a half later starlings were no longer considered "of use to the farmer." They had become an infestation:

Glen Ridge, N.J., Oct. 14, 1914 — The State Game and Fish Commission has given permission to the authorities of this borough to destroy the European starlings which have greatly amazed residents of several streets where the birds congregated in enormous numbers. Attempts of the residents to drive away the birds have been fruitless and they petitioned the local authorities to destroy them.

By 1928 the birds had reached the Mississippi River. Twenty years later they were in California. Through the decades the *Times* continued to document the invasion and our changing attitudes toward it:

December 20, 1931: "Baltimore has recently waged a defensive war against an army of starlings. Thousands of birds swooped down upon the city without warning..."

Jan 6, 1933: "An army of starlings estimated at 50,000 is making a night sanctuary of the Exterior of the Metropolitan Museum of Art, it was disclosed yesterday. The police regard this as a conservative estimate, and believe that [the number should be] 100,000 birds at least..."

July 9, 1933: "Like the English sparrow, the European starling is rolling up enemies by the score. Michigan farmers recently reported that thousands of starlings had settled in every county of the State. The huge flocks not only ravage the orchards, eating tons of fruit, but they commit a more serious offense, driving other birds out of their homes and sanctuaries."

By 1950 starlings had colonized North America from coast to coast and from Mexico to Hudson Bay, and ornithologists estimated the population in the United States had exceeded fifty million. (Today there are more than 200 million.)

> August 19, 1951: "The starlings and purple martins that have
> made nights hideous in a fashionable section here are getting a
> bitter taste of their own medicine—noise. Eddie Boyes, a Detroit
> radio engineer, is matching the starlings whistle for whistle and
> shriek for shriek and they don't like it."
> January 20, 1957: "Tenacious as office holders, persistent as
> lobbyists, insensitive as social climbers—all familiar types here—
> the starlings of Washington will not quit it."
> March 16, 1959: "Each day at sundown, motorists commuting over
> the Henry Hudson Parkway witness a 'black blizzard' of birds at
> 125th Street."

But our feelings are complex. When city workers in New York tried to reduce the pigeon population with poison, they inadvertently killed many starlings, awakening a surge of compassion:

> Dec 5, 1975: "A cluster of bird-lovers, some of them sobbing,
> gathered outside the Ethical Culture School at 33 Central Park
> West last night to mourn dozens of starlings, their feet mired in a
> chemical, that fell to their deaths from the school's roof..."

*

It's not clear how many birds Schieffelin and the American Acclimatization Society transported to America, but if they had Shakespeare's complete aviary in mind they probably fell short. Scholars have assembled an inventory of at least sixty-four birds mentioned in the plays and sonnets. The inventory includes blackbird, bunting, cormorant, crow, cuckoo, dove, duck, eagle, falcon, finch, goose, gull, and guinea hen. It includes also hedge sparrow, heron, jay, kestrel, kingfisher, kite, lapwing, lark, loon, magpie, mallard, nightingale, osprey, ostrich, and owl. There's mention, too, of "paraquito" (parakeet), parrot, partridge, peacock, pelican, pheasant, pigeon, quail, raven, rook, snipe, swallow, swan, thrush, vulture, woodcock, and wren. A starling appears just once in all of Shakespeare. It's in *Henry IV, Part I* (Act I, Scene III), in a scene in which the angry Hotspur, wishing to torment Henry, conceives the idea of having a starling repeat the name of the king's brother-in-law over and over. He says:

> But I will find him when he lies asleep,
> And in his ear I'll hollow "Mortimer!"
> Nay, I'll have a starling shall be taught to speak
> Nothing but "Mortimer," and give it him
> To keep his anger still in motion.

Shakespeare knew, of course, that starlings are excellent mimics and that they can sometimes be taught to speak a few words.

*

Every spring the giant sugar maple at the center of our yard becomes a starling hotel, its knot-hole rooms available by the week or month. Starlings take over the tree so completely that the ordinarily fearless red squirrels that claim it for their winter quarters hardly dare climb the trunk. The moment they get near the tree a dozen starlings mob them and they wisely retreat.

Often during baby-bird season, we find nestlings squirming on the lawn, where they've fallen from their cubby-hole nests twenty feet above. Many are dead when we find them, but one day we discovered two that were apparently unhurt. They were nearly fledged, about half the size of adults, and were struggling vainly to climb the trunk toward home and safety. We didn't have a ladder high enough to help, so the boys and I placed the terrified nestlings together in a makeshift nest, placed it in a cardboard box, and carried them inside the house.

Since childhood I had wanted to raise starlings and teach them to mimic a few words or even a few phrases of music, as Mozart was said to have done with his own pet starling. But it quickly became obvious that these two—my sons named them Beavis and Butthead—were not interested in experiments in vocalization. Nor were they interested in the bits of ground beef and other foods we tried to feed them. Finally we took them back outside, set them in their nest on the lawn beneath the tree, and retreated inside the house to watch through the windows. Within minutes an adult starling fluttered to the ground and shoved a cluster of larvae into Beavis's yawning mouth, then flew off. We have cats in the neighborhood, as well as fox, opossum, raccoon, crow, and other opportunistic eaters of nestlings, so I went outside and placed the nest and the young birds on a bird-feeder platform on a post well above the ground. Again, within minutes, an adult was there, stuffing food down their throats.

A gray squirrel began climbing the post with possible criminal intent and was instantly mobbed by three adult starlings. The birds made terrifying alarm calls and swooped in rapid, strafing dives. The squirrel, who was no fool, leaped for the walnut tree nearby and was chased half a dozen times around the trunk by a tightly banking starling.

Not long ago I watched a flock of thirty starlings land in the high weeds next to my office and disappear utterly. One moment they were dropping from the sky in a mass of flashing wings, and the next they were gone. I stepped outside for a better look and the entire flock rose at once. Their combined wingbeats made a rushing sound, like a sudden shower of rain, or like the spray from a garden sprinkler as it comes around. The flock climbed, switched, switched again, then flowed in an undulating stream across the meadow to Warren's oak tree. And when they reached the tree they disappeared again.

10
A MURMURATION OF STARLINGS

Starlings are a scourge on native birds, they spread disease, they steal mountains of grain and cost us plenty. It was a thick-headed decision to carry them across the world and release them. We know that now. But they're here to stay, so we might as well accept them. And the fact is, they're interesting—and they can surprise us with their beauty. Examine one up close or through binoculars and you'll see their plumage is stippled with stars that appear to be strewn across a background of black and iridescent purple. But let's skip the gothic beauty and get to the phenomenon that has inspired millions of YouTube viewers: their murmurations.

A few years ago I was driving along I-75 near Bay City, Michigan, in the agricultural flatlands of the Saginaw Valley. Across an expanse of fields, at a distance of perhaps a mile, I saw what at first I thought was a storm cloud or perhaps a plume of dark smoke hanging low in the sky. Then I realized that it was a cloud composed of birds—a single flock containing thousands or tens of thousands of starlings. In North America such flocks often include a scattering of red-winged blackbirds, cowbirds, grackles, sparrows, and other birds, but almost certainly they are comprised mostly of starlings.

This flock was extraordinary. First, it was vast: a warehouse-load of birds, a stadium's worth. It was too far away to pick out individual birds, which made the aggregate smokelike, a thick black swirling cloud of bird-smoke. It drifted in slow whorls above the field, curving and swirling as if stirred by a gigantic mixing spoon. The scene was so striking that I pulled onto the shoulder of the highway and got out of my car for a better look. The flock would pause for a moment, as if suspended, then sweep downward, pause again, and suddenly reverse direction and climb higher than before. At moments there were cross-swirls and vortexes within the flock, like the dust-devils that follow a car down a dirt road. It was mesmerizing.

Then I noticed a larger object plummeting through the cloud of birds: a hawk. It plunged into the smaller birds like a barracuda into a school of minnows. In its efforts to avoid the hawk the flock morphed into a shape like a donut, with the hawk passing through the hole. Something about its shape reminded me of three-dimensional drawings I've seen. Maybe illustrations of Einstein's concept of curved space. Maybe artists' renditions of galaxies being sucked into black holes. The hawk turned and climbed for another assault, then dived again, and the flock switched and turned, forming graceful, shifting, spiral-like shapes that geometry has not yet named.

What makes congregations of this sort stay together? How can birds in a flock or fish in a school make such sudden and apparently simultaneous switches, dives, and swoops without the individuals crashing into one another? Is there an intelligence at work? A theory popular a century ago, that a leader signals orders to the flock like a drum major at the head of a marching band, was disproved when high-speed photography revealed that the flocks constantly change leaders. More recent studies have focused on mathematical chaos theory, an approach that was pioneered by zoologist Frank Heppner, who studied flocking synchronism for many years. Heppner's computer programs animated collections of figures on the screen to represent birds, their motion closely duplicating the actual flight behavior of flocking birds. Software engineer Craig Reynolds famously designed a more complex computer model using what he called "Boids" to simulate the behavior of birds in a flock or fish in a school. Reynolds' "Boids" created flocks on the screen that exhibited such lifelike behavior that they've been put to use in Hollywood movies—to duplicate a swarm of bats, for instance, in Tim Burton's *Batman Returns*.

Of course there's another side to all of this. We can consider the scientific explanations—position and velocity, the various stimuli and responses, the binary codes of behavior, the need for individuals in a flock to remain close enough together to be safe from predators but far enough apart to avoid injury—and it helps us to understand the world, in the sense that it's probably not bewitchment we're witnessing or the gods idly stirring their swizzle sticks. We're reminded that the world is an unfolding story. It's the story of predators and prey, of sky and field and thermal updrafts and a horizon blazing red at sunset. It's the story of invasive species, of superhighways cutting across the land, of us now and then pulling off the highway in our efforts to notice a thing or two.

*

A murmuration of starlings, as most people know, is a congregation of starlings in flight. Most people also know that the word is one of many collective nouns or nouns of assembly that designate groups of animals. What is less known is that many of those words go back centuries, to an era when the aristocratic classes of Europe cultivated mannerisms and ways of speaking that could separate them from the common herd.

Some collective nouns began as "terms of venery" used in the hunting traditions of England and France during the fourteenth and fifteenth centuries. Rattling off those terms was a fashionable mark of erudition. The popular and often plagiarized *Book of Saint Albans*, first published in 1486 and authored in part, at least, by Dame Juliana Berners, included a long list of terms of venery for animals of interest to hunters and falconers. They included a "gaggle" of geese, a "mob" of deer, a "dole" of doves, a "covey" of grouse, a "bevy" of quail, a "fall" of woodcock, and a "sounder" of wild boar.

Many other terms were intended to be humorous. They included a "blush" of boys, a "hastiness" of cooks, a "pity" of prisoners, a "superfluity" of nuns, an "impertinence" of peddlers, a "drunkship" of cobblers, and a "melody" of harpists. Among the clever designations for groups of animals were a "shrewdness" of apes, a "pride" of lions, a "cowardice" of curs, an "exultation" of larks, and a "murder" of crows.

For starlings there were two terms: a "chattering" and a "murmuration." If you've ever been near a flock of starlings while they're occupied on the ground feeding or roosting in a tree or strung close to one another along a telephone line, you know they are vocal. They squeal. They grunt. Sometimes they chuckle. But mostly they murmur. You could say they chatter, but "murmuration" is perfect.

*

In nature, sometimes, everything fits. But seen another way it's pure chaos. In our search for synthesis in the world we notice patterns that when seen from a distance appear orderly. Photograph a leaf in extreme close-up and it passes for abstract art. Zoom out far enough and our sun is just one star in a vast, swirling galaxy of stars.

Stars are stipples. Starlings in a flock are stipples. The guy who released the first starlings into Central Park was a stipple. So are you and I.

That day, standing beside my car on the shoulder of I-75 watching that flock of starlings make fluid swoops in the distance, I became more aware than usual of the river of phenomena that flows around us every moment of our lives. I glimpsed the face of a young woman as she drove past, heard the blare of a horn, saw a flash of sunlight reflected off a windshield. I noticed that cars and trucks as they passed created little maelstroms of wind that rocked my car on its suspension. It occurred to me that our lives are made of moments that cluster together, like flocks. If we step back far enough we can sometimes see a pattern, and sometimes it is beautiful.

ECTOPISTES
MIGRATORIUS
1914
DRAWING FROM
A SPECIMEN IN
THE MSU MUSEUM
COLLECTION·1991

11
FROM A HILLTOP, LOOKING BACK

"For one species to mourn the death of another is a new thing under the sun."
—Aldo Leopold, *A Sand County Almanac*

Not so long ago, the high, grassy hill overlooking our little city was a good place to gain perspective on the world. On spring days you could drive up a gravel road, park in a meadow, and climb a short distance to the peak for an expansive and unobstructed view of the sky above and the town below. If you went there often enough, you could watch the seasons change—could watch spring change the trees below from mauve to green, watch the summer peak and fade, watch winter retreat up the bay to Lake Michigan, north toward Lake Superior and the Canadian wilderness.

From that hilltop you could witness the approach of thunderheads and misty streamers of rain, see squalls pierced by beams of sunlight long before they blundered across the lowlands. You could also see the corridors of industry, the new roads, the geometric patterns of subdivisions creeping up the slopes.

Without hilltops we can't see valleys. Without long views we're blind. Sometimes, from a hilltop, it's possible to see across centuries.

In the late 1800s people climbed that very hill above my hometown to watch vast flocks of passenger pigeons on their spring migration to northern Michigan. To those of us who have never seen a passenger pigeon, the stories about the numbers that once inhabited the central and eastern United States appear to be outrageous hyperbole. As early as the beginning of the seventeenth century, Samuel de Champlain and other early European explorers of the New World commented on the pigeons they encountered in "thickened clowdes" of "countless" or "infinite" number. They wrote of flocks so vast they blackened the sky for hours on end and contained so many individuals that when the birds settled in forests to roost their combined weight broke the limbs from trees. Observers claimed to have seen flocks containing millions, even billions, of pigeons. How could so many have existed? More crucially, how could they have disappeared?

John James Audubon was fascinated by the "wild pigeons" so common in his adopted home of Kentucky. In *Birds of America* he described a bird similar in appearance to the mourning dove, with a bluish head and back and a throat and breast the color of red wine, with wings and body designed for long migrations at speeds up to sixty miles per hour. But it was their sheer numbers that made the most powerful impression on Audubon.

"The multitudes of Wild Pigeons in our woods are astonishing," he wrote. "Indeed, after having viewed them so often, and under so many circumstances, I even now feel inclined to pause and assure myself that what I am going to relate is fact. Yet I have seen it all, and that too in the company of persons who, like myself, were struck with amazement."

In the autumn of 1813, Audubon witnessed a mile-wide flock of pigeons near Louisville, Kentucky, that passed overhead, without interruption, from noon until sunset and so filled the sky that daylight "was obscured as by an eclipse." By his estimate that single flock, one of dozens he saw that season, contained more than a billion birds (1,015,036,000, to be exact).

Another ornithologist, Alexander Wilson, in 1806 visited a pigeon breeding area in Kentucky that measured forty miles long and from one to three miles wide. Each of the trees within the breeding ground held as many as a hundred nests, and the surrounding ground was covered with broken branches, smashed eggs, and dead squabs. He estimated the area contained more than 2.23 billion birds.

The naturalist John Muir was fascinated with the life history of the bird and the beauty he perceived in them. In his memoir, *My Boyhood and Youth*, he recalls the flocks of passenger pigeons his family encountered after emigrating from Scotland to Wisconsin in 1849:

> I have seen flocks streaming south in the fall so large that
> they were flowing over from horizon to horizon in an almost
> continuous stream all day long, at the rate of forty or fifty miles
> an hour, like a mighty river in the sky, widening, contracting,
> descending like falls and cataracts, and rising suddenly here
> and there in huge ragged masses like high-plashing spray...
> They arrived in Wisconsin in the spring just after the sun had
> cleared away the snow, and alighted in the woods to feed on
> the fallen acorns that they had missed the previous autumn. A
> comparatively small flock swept thousands of acres perfectly
> clean of acorns in a few minutes, by moving straight ahead with
> a broad front. All got their share, for the rear constantly became
> the van by flying over the flock and alighting in front, the entire
> flock constantly changing from rear to front, revolving something
> like a wheel with a low buzzing wing roar that could be heard a
> long way off. In summer they feasted on wheat and oats and were
> easily approached as they rested on the trees along the sides of the
> field after a good full meal, displaying beautiful iridescent colors
> as they moved their necks backward and forward when we went

very near them. Every shotgun was aimed at them and everybody
feasted on pigeon pies, and not a few of the settlers feasted also
on the beauty of the wonderful birds. The breast of the male is a
fine rosy red, the lower part of the neck behind and along the sides
changing from the red of the breast to gold, emerald green and
rich crimson. The general color of the upper parts is grayish
blue, the under parts white. The extreme length of the bird is
about seventeen inches; the finely modeled slender tail about
eight inches, and extent of wings twenty-four inches. The females
are scarcely less beautiful. "Oh, what bonnie, bonnie birds!" we
exclaimed over the first that fell into our hands... It's awfu' like a
sin to kill them!"

Even as late as 1870, when much of the pigeon population had
been reduced by market hunting and habitat destruction, witnesses near
Cincinnati saw a single flock estimated to be a mile wide and 320 miles
long. Various observers have calculated that at one time the population of
passenger pigeons probably exceeded three billion, and that they would
have accounted for 25 to 40 percent of the total population of all the
birds in the United States.

It was their sheer abundance that was the species' undoing. Market
hunting was a common means of supplementing income in regions where
the pigeons were found, and few people worried that the population
could be seriously diminished by shotguns or nets. Even Audubon,
witnessing the wholesale killing of the birds, concluded that "no apparent
diminution ensues."

In 1831 Audubon described a scene along the Green River in
Kentucky, where local hunters had gathered at dusk to intercept flocks as
they returned to their roost:

The noise which they made, though yet distant, reminded me of
a hard gale at sea passing through the rigging of a close-reefed
vessel. As the birds arrived, and passed over me, I felt a current of

air that surprised me. Thousands were soon knocked down by the pole-men [swinging long poles to strike the flying birds]. The birds continued to pour in. The fires were lighted, and a magnificent, as well as wonderful and almost terrifying sight presented itself. The pigeons, arriving by thousands, alighted everywhere, one above another, until solid masses as large as hogsheads were formed on the branches all round. Here and there the perches gave way under the weight with a crash, and falling to the ground, destroyed hundreds of the birds beneath, forcing down the dense groups with which every stick was loaded. It was a scene of uproar and confusion. I found it quite useless to speak, or even to shout to those persons who were nearest to me. Even the reports of the guns were seldom heard, and I was made aware of the firing only by seeing the shooters reloading.... It was then that the authors of this devastation began their entry among the dead, the dying, and the mangled. The Pigeons were picked up and piled in heaps until each had as many as he could possibly dispose of, when the hogs were let loose to feed on the remainder.

Such killing was too widespread and too relentless to continue without consequences. Pigeons were shot, netted or clubbed wherever they congregated. Commercial netters took huge numbers by baiting small clearings with grains or salt, waiting until pigeons settled in the space to feed, then launching nets over them. Gunners frequently killed dozens of massed birds with a single shot. At a nesting sight near Shelby, Michigan, one trapper admitted killing and selling 175,000 pigeons himself during the spring of 1874. He estimated that in one thirty-day period he and the other trappers in Shelby killed and shipped an average of 100 barrels of birds per day—with 500 birds in every barrel—to restaurants in Chicago and Detroit. A total of 1.5 million pigeons would have been packed and shipped during those thirty days.

By the late 1800s, the birds were threatened both by commercial hunting and the clear-cutting of the hardwood forests where they nested and fed. The massive flocks were forced to move farther and farther north to find places where they could nest unmolested, and in the harsher climate may have fallen victim to late snow storms and cold spells, or may have perished when they were caught in storms over open water. Suddenly, almost before anyone could imagine it happening, the great flocks were gone.

Attempts were made to save them, but the efforts were too few and too late. The Michigan legislature in 1897 passed a law that prohibited the killing of passenger pigeons, but that was ten years after anyone had seen a sizable flock in the state. In the years after 1890 sightings of even a few pigeons anywhere in the United States had been notable enough to be mentioned in ornithological journals. Several flocks of four to six birds each were seen during the summer of 1893 at Elk River, Minnesota; in 1894 a flock of 500 was reported in Aitken County, Minnesota; and individual birds were spotted in Michigan's Upper Peninsula in 1895 and in southern Wisconsin in 1896. Just three years after Michigan passed its well-meaning but futile legislation to protect the birds, the last confirmed wild pigeon in the U.S. was shot and killed by a young boy in Pike County, Ohio.

Efforts to establish nesting populations in captivity were never successful. Audubon in 1830 shipped live birds across the Atlantic to a British nobleman, who managed a small flock for a number of years before it died out. A male and female captured in Wisconsin in 1888 eventually produced fifteen offspring, but, weakened by inbreeding, they all died by 1910.

In 1813, when Audubon counted 163 enormous flocks of pigeons pass overhead in twenty-one minutes, he was moved to predict that nothing could threaten the survival of this incredibly abundant species. Yet in fewer than a hundred years, the great flocks were gone forever, and the only remaining passenger pigeon on Earth was a single female, named for Martha Washington, at the Cincinnati Zoological Garden. Although it has been widely reported that Martha was born in captivity and lived to the age of twenty-nine, those facts are not certain. She was also said to have been born in the wild in Wisconsin, and to have been from seventeen to twenty-eight years old.

It is relatively certain, nonetheless, that Martha was the last passenger pigeon. None have been seen since she died in the Cincinnati Zoo on the afternoon of September 1, 1914.

Now we know, of course, that we're living in the midst of an age of mass extinctions, a "sixth extinction," as Elizabeth Kolbert calls it in her 2014 book of that title. The first of the previous five mass extinctions so far identified occurred 450 million years ago. Called the Ordovician-Silurian extinction, it resulted when glaciers across much of the planet locked up so much water that sea levels dropped precipitously, wiping out trilobites, brachiopods, and many other marine organisms. The deadliest of the events was the Permian-Triassic extinction event 250 million years ago, in which 90 percent of all species were eradicated, probably as a result of impact from asteroids or comets or from a series of massive volcanic eruptions. The most recent of the events was the Cretaceous Period extinction of sixty-five million years ago. Probably caused by dust and other debris that blanketed the earth after a massive asteroid struck near Mexico's Yucatan Peninsula, and perhaps amplified by a series of volcanic explosions in India, it killed the dinosaurs and three-quarters of all other animals.

Our current extinction event is one of the most devastating in the planet's history, and one that many scientists think will lead to the elimination of as many as 30 percent of all land and marine animals by the year 2030 and half of them by 2100, a rate of extinction and scale of loss unequalled since the Cretaceous Period. The event we're living through differs from previous events because it is caused by *homo sapiens,* a new agent of change on the planet, and it is taking place within a comparatively tiny sliver of the earth's time scale, one that geologists call the Holocene, "entirely recent," which extends from the last major ice age 11,700 years ago until today. Some scientists and environmentalists advocate naming our epoch the Anthropocene, the epoch of "new humans," because humans have made lasting and catastrophic impact on the planet—creating mass extinctions, altering the atmosphere, polluting the oceans, transforming landscapes. Some say the epoch should begin with the industrial revolution around 1800. Others say it should begin. 12,000 years ago, when we began producing our own food and plowing the land and otherwise altering the environment. Still others argue we should look back much further, to 200,000 years ago, when *homo sapiens* began migrating across the globe in cooperative groups and using stone weapons to hunt mastodons and other megafauna to extinction.

Regardless of when it began, the epoch of human impact is proceeding at an escalating rate. We're warming the climate. We're cutting down forests—including, most disastrously, the tropical rain forests where the greatest diversity of animals and plants is found. We're overfishing the oceans. We're poaching endangered animals for their tusks, meat, and other body parts. We're introducing invasive species around the world that eradicate native plants and animals. The result is not only one of the largest mass extinctions of all time, but one of the most rapid.

Nobody knows the exact rate at which animal and plant species are becoming extinct, but estimates range from as few as one to as many as several hundred per day. In some places, most notably the rain forests, where as many as two million species live in an area covering only seven percent of the total landmass of the planet, many organisms are vanishing before biologists have a chance to identify and name them, let alone study their roles in ecosystems.

Hundreds of insects, reptiles, fish, crustaceans, and plants disappear each year with little or no fanfare. Birds, mammals, and amphibians are the glamour species on the extinction list and are the ones most likely to make news. Those lost since the turn of the twenty-first century include the Pyrenean ibex of Spain and France; the Yantze River dolphin of China (declared "functionally" extinct since none have been seen since 2002); the golden toad of the Monteverde Cloud Forest in Costa Rica and Holdridge's toad of the Costa Rican rainforest; the Hawaiian crow (extinct in the wild, though a few dozen survive in captivity); the West African black rhino; the black-faced honeycreeper of Hawaii's island of

Maui (three of the birds were discovered alive in 1998, but none have been seen since 2004); the alaotra grebe of Madagascar (declared extinct in 2010, though none had been seen since 1982).

The question needs to be asked: so what? Why should we care if rain forests are cut down for their timber and to make agricultural fields? What difference does it make if plants and animals that have not yet been discovered and named should become extinct? Why should we care about the fate of a wildflower in South America or a songbird in Asia?

The biologist E.O. Wilson and others have identified three common reasons that people don't care and have answered them with arguments for why we should:

1. Extinction is natural and evolution will eventually replace lost species with new ones.

Answer: Yes, extinction is natural, but major extinction events are so devastating that we and most other species are unlikely to survive them. It took ten million years to restore lost biodiversity after each of the great extinction events of the past 400 million years.

2. We don't need millions of species. Who will miss spiders and houseflies?

Answer: Biologists and ecologists have established unequivocally that the more species there are living in an ecosystem, the greater is its ability to withstand drought, flooding, and other environmental stresses. A diverse ecosystem is a healthy, working one that produces the oxygen we breathe, cleans the water we drink, and enriches the soil that grow the food we eat.

Furthermore, at least 40 percent of the medicines we currently use are derived from wild plants, animals, fungi, and microorganisms. For example, aspirin, the most commonly used medicine in the world, was originally extracted from the meadowsweet plant, *Filpendula ulmaria*. To date only a tiny percentage of the world's flora have been tested for their medicinal and nutritional values. It's reasonable to presume that among those that have not yet been identified and studied are a few at least (and probably many) that will in one way or another improve our health and quality of life.

3. Why rush to save every species? Why not preserve them in zoos and botanical gardens and "seed" the wild with them if they should become endangered?

Answer: Because all the zoos can hold fewer than 10 percent of the known species of mammals, birds, amphibians, and reptiles, and even fewer of the 250,000 known plants. Smaller organisms present greater complications, since there is no certain way to keep them in captivity.

Some skeptics scoff at the idea that we have an ethical responsibility to protect earth's inhabitants, but nobody can deny that our lives would be immeasurably poorer without otters and warblers and cheetahs. Perhaps most important, no one knows the precise role each species plays in the larger scheme of things. All we know for certain is that all living things on the planet depend for their survival on associations with other living things. Individual species have been compared to the rivets that hold an airplane together. How long can the rivets keep popping before the plane comes crashing down?

If we can remember the lessons of the passenger pigeon, the great auk, the dodo, the sea mink, and the rufous gazelle, maybe we can direct our energies toward slowing further losses. Surely that's where our best hope lies. But it's difficult not to feel cheated.

The hill above our city was bought by developers years ago and is built over now with attractive houses, each with a view of the valley, the city, and the bay. I still go there sometimes, looking for perspective, but I can't stay for long. The view is so cluttered. The sky is so empty.

PART II

ANIMAL BEHAVIOR

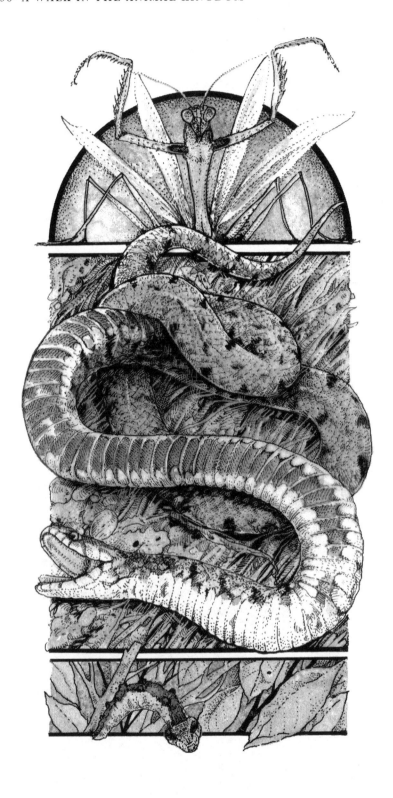

12
THE BEST DEFENSES

Things are not always what they seem. One morning in Michigan's Upper Peninsula my old friend Craig Date stepped from the bow of our canoe without paying much attention to where he was going and nearly stepped on a big, diamond-blotched, thick-as-a-forearm snake coiled on a rock. When the snake reared its head as if to strike and began a furious rattling, Craig did a nifty little backward leap into the canoe and in two bounds joined me in the stern.

After a few moments of confusion, while the canoe rocked from gunwale to gunwale and Craig and I rifled through our packs in search of a camera, we remembered that there aren't supposed to be venomous snakes in the Upper Peninsula. Cautious examination revealed that the busily rattling snake on the rock in front of us lacked a rattle on its tail. The buzzing sound was produced by the tip of the tail vibrating rapidly against some dry leaves. A herpetologist at Michigan State University later informed us that our "rattler" was a fox snake, a harmless species that if threatened often mimics the rattlesnake's aggressive behavior.

Evolutionary scientists since the age of Darwin have observed that defense against predators is one of the most—if not *the* most—powerful influences on natural selection. In a world of hunters and hunted, the latter have evolved a dazzling array of tactics to increase their chances of survival. These tactics range from the intriguing to the downright unbelievable. It is little wonder people have so frequently been bamboozled into believing tales of porcupines shooting their quills with arrowlike accuracy and snakes hurling themselves like javelins at attackers.

Biologists divide the dozen or so major types of animal defenses into two categories, the primary and the secondary. Primary defenses are those that are present whether predators are around or not and include camouflage, aposematism (advertising with bright colors or other signals that they possess dangerous or unpleasant qualities), mimicry of distasteful or poisonous animals, and living in groups, burrows, cavities, cases, and shells.

When an animal is threatened or attacked and its primary defenses fail, it may turn to more active, secondary defenses, such as fleeing, adopting intimidating or threatening postures, feigning death, deflecting attack, or retaliating. The wasp's black and yellow coloration is a primary defense and its sting a secondary one. The shell of a tortoise is a primary defense; drawing its head and legs inside is a secondary one.

The fox snake Craig nearly stepped on was employing one of the simplest and most common secondary defenses in the animal world: the threat display. By greatly inflating lungs, spreading wings, fluffing feathers or fur, or otherwise making themselves appear larger, animals such as toads, mantises, and nesting birds make themselves appear as menacing as possible in hopes of frightening away predators. These threat displays are effective only because the world is so full of genuine warnings. A skunk raises its tail and then rears its hind legs before spraying; a cobra flares its neck; arctiid moths open their wings to display bright markings on their abdomens before exuding a nauseating fluid from their thoraxes.

One of the most familiar and amusing secondary displays is the hognose snake's. When threatened this stout North American snake gives every indication of being a ferocious killer. It opens its mouth, hisses, "hoods" its head, rears back, and strikes. If you call its bluff, however—and it's an easy bluff to call, because the snake is harmless—it will immediately flip over and pretend to be dead. The snake takes its death scene so seriously that if you turn it over onto its belly it will promptly flip onto its back again.

The hognose snake's feigned death is a tactic known as thanatosis, and is used by a number of animals—including some beetles, spiders, domestic fowl, bobwhite quail, ducks, rabbits, and primates—usually as a last resort if the animal's other defenses have failed to be effective. Another snake capable of a convincing death performance is the common grass snake of Europe. Confronted by a predator, it will hiss, stick out its tongue, regurgitate or defecate, fake rigor mortis, and, as a grotesque finale, cut loose with stink glands that emit an odor said to smell like a mixture of mouse droppings and garlic.

Impressive as such performances can be, few animals play possum as convincingly as the opossum itself, which not only flops over onto its side, goes limp, and lets its tongue loll, but also defecates and emits a foul-smelling ooze from its anal glands. In addition, its metabolism slows dramatically. Unlike most death-feigners, the opossum has been known to stay "dead" for lengthy periods—up to six hours, in some cases.

As a child, I spent a lot of time walking along the beaches around Lake Michigan, and I can remember being baffled when a killdeer or piping plover ran ahead of me, keening in distress and dragging one wing, apparently able to fly only in fluttering hops. I would follow, concerned and curious. The bird would fall, fluttering pathetically, its wings outstretched as if broken, yet always managing to keep a safe distance ahead of me. After a while, the bird, as if suddenly cured of it injury, would fly off. Of course I was witnessing an elaborate performance intended to lure a potential predator away from the bird's camouflaged but otherwise vulnerable nest. Predators are often unable to resist chasing an injured bird and will run blindly after it. Once the predator is safely away from the nesting site, the adult bird can circle back and resume incubating its eggs or feeding its young.

For animals such as antelopes, otters, and roadrunners that are skilled at running, jumping, swimming, or flying, the obvious defensive strategy is to flee. Others have to be more creative. The larva of the North American argus tortoise beetle collects its own excrement and carries it in a pouch formed from old molted skin on its back. When an ant or other predator approaches, the larva swings the "bag," called a fecal shield, between it and the predator. Thomas Eisner, an entomologist at Cornell University, found that when ants bit into the bag or were smeared with excrement from it, they usually retreated and left the larva unharmed.

Predators themselves are often fair game and must depend on a variety of defenses of their own. Ornithologist Dr. William Scharf, formerly of the University of Nebraska, notes that the sideburnlike marks on the head of an American kestrel are suggestive of the eyes of an owl and might prevent larger raptors from attacking the small falcon.

The spinifex striped gecko of Australia can shoot a thick, sticky liquid from its tail. Accurate at a distance of up to two feet, the liquid entangles predators in a kind of cobweb, slowing and distracting them long enough to allow the gecko to escape. If threatened from the front, the gecko opens its mouth suddenly, revealing a shocking orange interior that may startle a predator and cause it to retreat.

Another way to deter an attacker is to throw it a sacrifice. Many lizards depend on a mechanism called autotomy, or "self amputation," to escape a predator that has grasped them by their tails: The tail simply breaks off. The predator gets some reward for its effort—the tail is edible—and the lizard escapes with its life.

If all else fails, disgust a predator. The Atlantic hagfish, or slime eel, is an eel-like fish found on the muddy bottom of ocean waters from the western Mediterranean to the coast of North America, where it feeds on dead fish and other organisms. It has the strange ability to tie itself into a knot to escape a predator's grip, but its main defense is its ability to exude massive amounts of thick, slimy mucus from glands the length of its body. In the ensuing mess, the hagfish wriggles free and escapes.

An animal can sometimes escape a predator by startling it with sudden and unexpected behavior. A ruffed grouse, erupting from the undergrowth, beats the air with cupped wings that create a noise loud enough to momentarily disorient a fox or coyote. Most of the 200-or-so species of underwing moths in North America, Europe, and Asia are nocturnal feeders that spend the perilous daylight hours hiding, camouflaged on trunks or branches of trees. When discovered by a bird such as the blue jay, the moth flares its wings to reveal colorful patterns that will often startle the bird into flight. "Eyespots" on the underwings of the Io moth resemble the eyes of owls and apparently triggers a bird's fear of predators. In the ensuing moments of confusion, the moth can relocate and hide again.

The snake caterpillar, the larva of a neotropical hawkmoth, has one of the strangest startle responses. When threatened, the caterpillar swings its head toward the source of the threat and expands it into what looks like the head of a small snake, complete with large, dark eyes. The performance is so convincing that a bird or other small predator will usually veer away.

Nick and his friend Dan once discovered a praying mantis in our yard. The boys ran to me shouting that they had found a "big green bug with big legs and claws." Their alarm was understandable, considering that a mantis, when threatened, expends a good deal of effort making itself appear more dangerous than it is. The boys and I got down on our knees in the grass to examine the creature. I poked a finger at it and it reared back ready to strike with the sharp spines and claws on its forelegs, at the same time exposing bright eyespots on the insides of its legs and rotating its head on its flexible neck to keep my finger in view. When I persisted, it flared its wings to make itself look even larger and more imposing.

The nineteenth-century French entomologist J. Henri Fabre called the female praying mantis "the tigress of the peaceable entomological tribes, the ogress in ambush who levies a tribute of fresh meat." With its efficient green camouflage, a convincing threat display, and the retaliating sharpness of those foreleg spines, this formidable hunter of insects is itself well defended against predators.

Dan wanted to show the mantis to his parents, so we captured it in a jar and he ran home across the meadow carrying it before him. When he reached home his big brother promptly relieved him of the jar, shook the mantis into his hand, and fed it to his pet turtle. Nature, red in tooth and claw, bristling with innovative defenses, is still no match for small boys with slingshots.

13
STINGS AND ARROWS

I'm not sure what kind of jellyfish it was that I brushed against that day on the Atlantic coast of Florida. A two-day blow had pushed Portuguese men-of-war, cannonball jellyfish, and sea nettles to the shore, so it could have been any of them. Authorities had been warning swimmers to stay out of the water, but nobody was paying attention to them.

Some jellyfish billow in the water like a pair of Victorian bloomers; others are nearly transparent and difficult to spot; still others are as elaborately colored as tropical orchids. Biologists group all of them with corals and sea anemones in a 10,000-plus-member phylum, Cnidaria, which means "stinging thread," referring to the animals' tentacles. Each tentacle is armed with thousands of nematocysts, or stinging cells, which, when touched, fire tiny coiled darts that release venom that can paralyze small prey in seconds. This is such a formidable defense system—imagine coils of concertina wire tipped with hypodermic needles filled with acid—that only loggerhead turtles and a few other predators are willing to pay the price of eating jellyfish.

That day in the Florida surf I was treading water, waiting for the next big wave, when two searing, white-hot jolts of pain struck my ankle—

Bam! Bam!—like a double whammy from a wasp. I limped from the water and, following the advice of a nearby surfer, scooped up a handful of wet sand and rubbed the afflicted area vigorously. It helped a little. I remember looking at the ocean with new appreciation.

Luckily for me, most North American jellyfish inflict a painful sting but are not dangerous. In the waters off northern Australia, however, lives a species of nearly transparent box jellyfish known as the sea wasp, whose nine-foot-long tentacles are covered with millions of cnidocytes that are loaded with deadly venom. The sea wasp does not kill often—most sources report an average of about one fatality per year in Australia's waters—but swimmers who become entangled in a mass of the tentacles can be stung so severely that they die in only two or three minutes.

The coast of northern Australia is home also to some of the most venomous of all fishes, the stonefishes. Stonefishes and their close relatives scorpionfishes inhabit reefs and the bottoms of intertidal shallows. Some species are flamboyant and colorful; others are camouflaged to blend in with rocks and coral. All tend to be small and fiercely armed. The Australian stonefish is a warty camouflage artist that supports forests of algae on its back and spends most of its time hiding motionless among rocks, coral, and bottom rubble. Its fins carry sharp spines, each with two sacs containing a collective ten milligrams of a potent venom. Those who have stepped on a stonefish report pain so severe that it can cause hallucinations. Very rarely a severe case will be fatal.

In most parts of the world, barefoot and carefree is a bad way to go. Hikers and rock climbers are taught not to place their hands on unseen ledges or jump to spots they cannot see. Divers in the ocean are instructed never to touch an unfamiliar creature and never to reach into a dark cranny. They could be pierced by fangs, stabbed by tails, spiked by spines, or slashed by razorlike protuberances. They could be poisoned.

The terms *venomous* and *poisonous* are sometimes used interchangeably, but venomous properly refers to any animal that injects its venom into a victim. A plant or animal is poisonous if it sickens someone who ingests it or touches it. Jellyfish, cobras, and scorpions are venomous. The deadly nightshade plant and poison dart frogs are poisonous.

One of the difficulties in identifying poisonous organisms is that there are so many myths and so much wrong information attached to them. Many people assume, for example, that it is safe to eat a berry or a plant if they see wildlife eating it. That is most definitely not the case. Some animals have natural immunity to toxins that are dangerous to humans. Many birds, for example, eat the berries of poison ivy, while deer, mice, and rabbits routinely nibble the stems and leaves. A squirrel can safely eat the mushroom *Amanita muscaria*, which is potentially dangerous and occasionally fatal to people.

Venom makes it possible for small or slow-moving predators, such as some snakes, insects, spiders, centipedes, shrews, octopuses, and even a few snails, to capture prey that is larger and faster than they. The venom is often produced in modified salivary glands linked by ducts to hollow or grooved fangs or teeth. Other animals, such as scorpions, are equipped with venomous stingers on the ends of their abdomens. Some venomous animals and virtually all poisonous plants use toxins strictly for defense. These animals include the platypus, with its venom-pumping spur, and sea urchins, bees, wasps, some caterpillars, some fishes, and at least one species of salamander. Those that use poison more passively include toads and frogs and a few fishes, all of which secret toxins from glands in their skin. Some insects, such as the monarch butterfly, concentrate toxins in their bodies from the plants they eat, making them inedible. Hedgehogs have been known to capture toads and rub them on their own spikes to cover themselves with toxins.

Venomous animals produce three kinds of venom, often in combination: neurotoxins, which attack the nervous system and cause death by heart failure or suffocation; hemotoxins, which attack the circulatory system; and cardiotoxins, which directly affect the heart. Venoms probably began as digestive aids. Primitive snakes found it easier and more efficient to swallow prey whole than to tear it apart or chew it. Snakes with powerful digestive enzymes had an advantage, particularly if the enzymes could be introduced into the prey while it was still living and distributed through its body via its own circulatory system. Digestion could begin even before the prey was swallowed. Some of the salivary enzymes proved toxic to prey. The earliest venomous snakes were probably equipped with large, grooved teeth through which toxic saliva could be pumped into the tissues of a prey animal. Some of today's snakes have not evolved much beyond this early model.

Others, however, have developed more sophisticated venom systems. In the vipers, grooved teeth have become hollow fangs hinged to swing forward in a stabbing motion when biting. The impact of the stab pumps venom from enlarged glands through the fangs into the victim.

In most venomous animals, defense against enemies is an important benefit of having a bite that is worse than the bark. A painful bite is a harsh lesson not quickly forgotten, which is why venomous and poisonous animals often advertise themselves. Predators learn quickly that a red or yellow creature or one that rattles its tail or hisses in warning is not to be fooled with.

Unfortunately, venomous snakes don't always advertise themselves. The eastern diamondback, the largest and probably the most dangerous of North America's rattlesnakes, is especially unreliable with its rattles and may strike silently and without warning when startled or threatened. Baby rattlesnakes are venomous when they are less than twenty-four hours old, before their rattles develop. They are born with a "prebutton" that grows into a small button after they shed their skin for the first time, but it makes no sound. The venom in a baby rattler is drop for drop more potent than the venom found in mature snakes, but young snakes possess much less of it and inject relatively small amounts. Still, a bite from even a very small rattlesnake is painful and can be dangerous.

For most people, venomous snakes are represented by a single, terrifying image: fangs. That image endures even when we know that the chance of encountering fanged snakes are very small and the chance of dying from their bite is even smaller. In the United States, where about 500 people a year die from allergic reactions to bees and wasps and fewer than thirty are struck and killed by lighting, only about five people a year die from snake bites. Even fewer have fatal encounters with spiders, scorpions, Gila monsters, stingrays, jellyfish, and other venomous animals. Still, our fear of venomous bites goes deep. We apparently aren't born with it—toddlers will reach innocently for a snake—but we learn early and what we learn seems to awaken dormant terrors.

Yet, there's a kind of pleasure in the fear. We listen spellbound to a herpetologist telling us that the saw-scaled viper of Egypt, Israel, and the Arabian Peninsula is probably the most lethal of all snakes and that the bite of even a ten-inch specimen can be fatal. We're fascinated to learn that Myanmar (formerly Burma) is the world headquarters for dangerous snake bites, with about fifteen of every 100,000 people dying from bites annually; and that in India, where there are about fifty species of venomous snakes, 10,000 to 15,000 people die each year from bites.

Danger has a way of stirring up fears we may not even know we have until an electric surge of adrenalin jolts us to awareness. Such awareness has biological advantages. It's our best defense. Seeing death coiled six feet away alerts us to the moment, elevates our heartbeat, cranks our emergency system into the red zone—and makes us feel very, very alive.

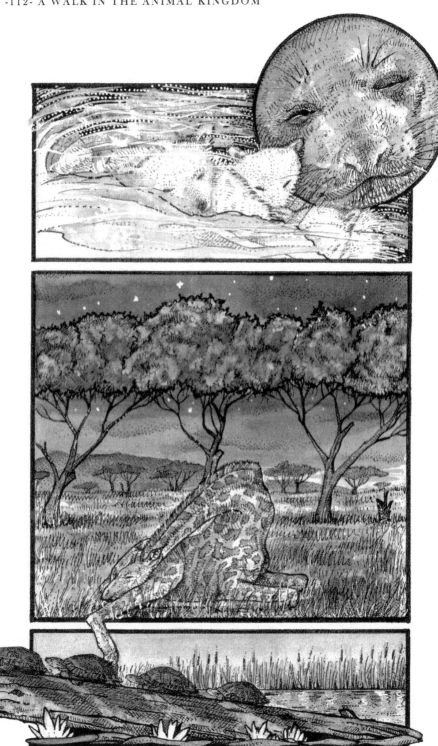

14
SLEEPY TIME

When I was in my energetic twenties I wished that I could be freed from the tyranny of sleep. It was one of my favorite subjects at parties. Think how productive we could be, I would say, how educated. We could pay our bills doing a paltry eight hours of work, then be free during the remaining sixteen hours to pursue our real interests. Think of the books we could read! The music we could master! The paintings to paint and poems to write! Think of the languages we could learn to speak if we applied ourselves in the otherwise wasted hours between midnight and dawn!

Be careful what you wish for. Now, as a sometime insomniac, I have many opportunities to practice French and Russian, but I squander every one. I pass the wee hours, instead, envying the easy sleep of puppies. Puppies drop into sleep as easily as stones drop into water. Several nights each week I drop partway, then dangle, suspended. An astrologer friend once explained that I, a Libra, am morbidly concerned with balance and have difficulty weighing day and night, wakefulness and sleep. She proposed that when my psychic scales reach harmony, I sleep; when they are in discord (as they usually are), I toss and turn.

If you're lucky, and have a clear conscience, you can count on spending approximately one-third of your life asleep. Yet for an activity that consumes such a significant portion of our time, we know remarkably little about it. Serious sleep research did not begin until the 1950s, when researchers at the University of Chicago first used electroencephalograph (EEG) machines, invented in 1929, to measure the brain-wave patterns of sleeping people and laboratory animals. They quickly learned that all animals undergo drastic bodily changes while sleeping. Muscles relax, breathing slows, body temperatures drop. But the most surprising discovery was that human sleep is broken into four stages, from lightest to deepest, alternating with periods when our bodies rest but our eyes are moving rapidly beneath their lids. During these periods of rapid-eye-movement, or REM, our brains are as active as if we were awake. Volunteers awakened during REM sleep usually report that they have been dreaming. EEG readings of other animals show that we share intervals of REM sleep with most mammals and at least some birds.

Most humans have adapted a pattern of *monophasic* sleep—sleeping for a single period every twenty-four hours. Yet that may not be the most natural pattern. According to some researchers, monophasic sleep may have originated to meet the demands of agricultural and industrial societies, contrary to our natural propensity for *polyphasic* sleep, or sleep that occurs more than once a day. Evidence of *biphasic*, or twice daily sleep patterns, can be seen in the now disappearing siesta cultures of some countries and in the fact that most sleep research subjects prove to have regular twelve-hour cycles, with maximum sleepiness occurring in both the middle of the night and the middle of the afternoon. In free-running experiments, when subjects have no clues as to what time it is and are allowed to sleep whenever they feel tired, most people split their sleep into two periods, a major one at night and a minor one in mid-afternoon. Such a pattern could be a relic of ages when humans who relied on animals for sustenance would have found it practical to be alert and hunting when their prey was most active, in morning and evening, and to be resting during the hottest part of the day, when many animals are inactive.

For all the stacks of information compiled about what happens during sleep, nobody is able to say with certainty why animals do it. Noted sleep researcher James Horne, author of the boldly titled book *Why We Sleep*, confesses early on that he does not know why we sleep. Nobody does. There are numerous theories—sleep keeps animals hidden from predators, conserves energy, restores the body and the brain, fills unproductive time, allows an outlet for dreaming—but none of them hold up under experiment as the complete answer. For most animals, in fact, sleep is downright dangerous. Even when hidden in burrows and nests, sleeping animals are far more vulnerable to predators than when awake. Considering the hectic agenda most animals must maintain to find enough food for themselves and their offspring, sleep seems like a considerable disadvantage. In a comment that may summarize the frustrations of many of his colleagues, sleep researcher Allan Rechtschaffen once said, "If sleep does not serve an absolutely vital function, then it is the biggest mistake the evolutionary process ever made."

The most obvious examples of that evolutionary error, if it is indeed an error, are found among large wildlife. If there was ever an animal that should have evolved a substitute for sleep, it is the giraffe. It takes about fifteen seconds for a giraffe to stand up, during which time it is dangerously subject to attack. In compensation, perhaps, giraffes sleep only about two hours out of every twenty-four hours, and even that sleep is broken up into naps. They have been observed to lie down from three to eight times each night, for periods ranging from three minutes to seventy-five minutes. And during most of those minutes, the giraffes are awake. If sleep wasn't essential, giraffes almost certainly would not bother with it.

Dolphins seem to have solved the problem of vulnerability by sleeping with one eye open at all times. Spinner dolphins in the open ocean feed and socialize most actively at night, when their ability to echolocate gives them an advantage over the sharks that prey on them. During late morning and early afternoon they rest by swimming slowly in groups in shallow, protected bays. Biologist Kenneth Norris, who spent more than twenty years observing and studying dolphins, reported in his book, *Dolphin Days*, that "sleep" might not be the right word for what dolphins do at rest, since they swim together sedately in slow, milling patterns, often in the company of regular sleeping partners and always with at least one eye open. Evidence from brain-wave measurements suggests dolphins have the remarkable ability to put only one hemisphere of their brains to sleep at a time. The tactic allows them to rest even while watching for sharks and other predators and while surfacing periodically for air.

Although there are few hard-and-fast rules when it comes to sleep, predators tend to sleep longer and sounder than prey animals. Canadian zoologist Ian Stirling notes in his book *Polar Bears* that during the summer polar bears sleep about a quarter of each day, although it is impossible to say for sure since the bears catch frequent brief naps while lying beside breathing holes waiting for seals to surface. More certain is the fact that the bears like to sleep an hour or two after eating and more often during the day than night, probably because seals, their primary prey, feed mostly at night and are most easily caught then. To sleep, polar bears dig shallow pits in the snow or ground and lay with their backs to the wind. Blowing snow will often cover them as they sleep. Adult females with cubs prefer to dig their pits high on hillsides, where they have a clear view of the surrounding country and are less likely to be surprised by marauding males that might prey on the cubs. Stirling kept track of seventeen sleep periods that lasted longer than an hour each, and found them to average seven hours and forty-five minutes each, about the same as the ideal length of human sleep.

The spiny anteater of Australia is one of only two mammals that lays eggs (the other is the duck-billed platypus). When hooked to an EEG machine, it was found to be the only mammal ever tested that shows no evidence of slipping into REM sleep. All other tested mammals alternate periods of active sleep and quiet sleep and are capable, in theory at least, of dreaming. Anyone who owns dogs is convinced they dream. It's common to see them enter periods of sleep during which their eyes move wildly beneath the lids and they jerk their legs and snort air, as if dreaming of running. "Chasing squirrels," we used to say of our overweight Labrador retriever, who was clearly incapable of catching one while awake.

It's difficult to measure the amount of time animals spend sleeping, since most are polyphasic, sleeping for many short periods each day. Amounts of sleep vary with individual, species, season, weather, latitude, and activities such as breeding and nesting. Nonetheless, biologists have a fairly good idea of how much sleep various animals get per day. They know that among mammals, roe deer get about 2.5 hours; horses and donkeys about three; guinea pigs about 9.5; rabbits about 14.5; cats about fifteen; bats and opossums about twenty. Elephant seals sleep from eight to ten hours each day, ceasing to breathe up to thirty minutes at a time while asleep. Measurements of the brain waves of house cats in soundproof cages indicate that they spend, on average, a little less than 8.5 hours per day awake, twelve hours in light sleep, and 3.5 hours in deep sleep. Humans perform most tasks best and are most alert when they get 7.5 to eight hours sleep, yet studies show that the average person in most industrial countries gets considerably less than that.

Among birds, ostriches sleep seven to nine hours each day; ducks, eleven hours; hawks and owls, twelve. While it is not known how much time most songbirds actually spend sleeping, researchers have measured the time they spend at rest and found it to vary greatly according to the season. Edward A. Armstrong watched a winter wren in Cambridge, England for one year and discovered that it rested about 18.5 hours in December (when cold temperatures and short days made it prudent to conserve energy) and about 7.5 hours in June. Observers have noted that above the Arctic Circle, during the continuous daylight of summer, snow buntings rest only three to five hours each day.

Birds tend to sleep in the same kinds of places that they nest. Songbirds that nest in trees are more likely to roost at similar heights, while species that nest on the ground are likely to roost there as well. When nights are cool, the Eurasian skylark and the horned lark of the western United

States dig shallow depressions in the soil with their bills. They spend the night nestled in the soil, with their exposed backs nearly level with the ground. Probably because birds that sleep on the ground are especially vulnerable, they tend to be more active at night and sleep less soundly than small songbirds that roost in shrubbery or trees.

Northern bobwhites form mutual defense leagues to sleep in relative security at night. Bobwhites in a covey arrange themselves in a tight circle, each bird facing out, pressed between the birds on either side. The arrangement conserves body heat and allows 360-degree surveillance. If approached, the covey bursts into flight, each bird flying away from the others in a sudden explosion of wings that startles and disorients predators. The instinct to arrange themselves in circles when resting is so strong that even day-old chicks do it.

In winter, ptarmigans and some grouse fly into loose snow drifts or burrow into the snow to spend the night relatively insulated from the cold. Likewise, snow buntings take cover in snowdrifts or in tiny crevices and depressions that protect them from wind. Willow tits in Siberia have been observed burrowing into the snow and sleeping in the abandoned burrows of rodents.

Pelagic birds—those that live mostly on or above the oceans—typically sleep while floating on the water, but a few species have had to forego that easy solution. If frigatebirds were to land on the sea, their plumage would quickly soak up so much water that they would drown. They avoid the problem by feeding on an airborne diet of flying fish, or by scooping up edible bits from the surface, or by poaching from other seabirds—harassing them in the air until they drop the food they carry, which the frigatebirds deftly snatch as it falls. When they're near land they roost for the night on bushes, but they are frequently seen so far from landfalls that it can be surmised that they sleep while gliding above the water. Likewise, the absorbent plumage of the sooty tern forces it to sleep on the wing.

The distinction between rest and sleep is not always clear, especially in cold-blooded animals. Some fish appear to sleep, others merely to rest. Among those most likely to sleep are the parrot fish, which secretes a protective covering of mucus and rests on the bottom. Others, like mackerel, which must swim constantly to keep water moving over their gills, appear never to sleep, although it is possible they are capable of short sleeplike episodes while in motion. Some reef fishes in Bermuda, when studied during periods of inactivity, showed evidence of entering brief episodes of REM sleep. Sharks of the open ocean appear never to sleep, or not in the sense mammals do, because to cease swimming would cause them to sink a mile or more. In shallow water, however, some shark species rest on the bottom, on rocky ledges, and even inside shallow caverns.

Reptiles and amphibians go through periods of sleeplike rest that some researchers theorize could be a primitive form of REM sleep. Crocodiles show brain-wave patterns that suggest sleep but give no sign of rapid eye movement. Bullfrogs observed around the clock seem never to sleep. Freshwater turtles can sleep submerged on the bottom of ponds or floating on the surface or lined up basking in the sun on exposed logs and rocks. Most snakes seek secluded, protected nooks to sleep, but some species of water snakes doze in the open, stretched out on branches or logs over water. If snakes are light sleepers, it is probably because they lack eyelids. Instead, snake eyes are covered with an immovable transparent tissue that allows them to detect nearby movement even while sleeping. It's difficult to sneak up on a snake.

All living things require rest. Studies have proven that people who get a solid eight hours of sleep each night live longer than sleepers who get less, yet we're always trying to get by on fewer hours. Part of the problem is that many of us try to keep up the pace set by prodigies like Thomas Edison, that hard-working chump, who bragged in public that he never got more than four or five hours of sleep—then admitted in his private journal that he often turned off his alarm and went back to sleep.

With diligent training, a few ambitious souls have managed to thrive on as little as two or three hours of sleep every day. Those people tend to give up the experiment eventually, not because they are tired, but because the days begin to drag on and on. I can report from many years of experience that the hours between two o'clock and four o'clock in the morning grow long indeed. As John Berryman might have said, life without sleep, friends, is boring.

15
TRACKS IN THE SAND

In a universe dominated by chaos and chance, there is sometimes order, balance, and harmony to all things. I know that's true, though most of the time I'm too distracted to notice and must accept balance and harmony on faith. But one night on Florida's Melbourne Beach, with a quarter moon low over the Atlantic and loud, plunging breakers lighting the surf with lines of foam, there was rare symmetry in the sand. Sea turtles—those ancient, enigmatic, and imperiled inhabitants of open ocean and night-shrouded tropical beaches—were hard at work being born. And life on the narrow shore was in balance with the vast, life-giving waters of the sea.

It began with a female loggerhead turtle crawling from the water onto shore. Loggerheads, named for their large blockish skulls, are the most common of the sea turtles found along Florida's coast. They are the most common, but far from abundant. All five genera of sea turtles inhabiting the North Atlantic—the leatherbacks, greens, ridleys, hawksbills, and loggerheads—have suffered exploitation. For centuries they've been harpooned, netted, shot, or captured on beaches. They've been butchered wholesale for steaks and soup and stacked belly-up on the decks of ships as living larder during long ocean journeys. Their eggs are gathered to supply illicit markets hungry for easy protein and rumored aphrodisiacs. Coastal development has destroyed countless beaches where adult females once came ashore to nest. The result is that all the turtles of the oceans are in danger of extinction. Loggerheads are luckier than most, merely threatened.

Once nesting as far north in the Atlantic as Virginia, loggerheads have been pushed progressively farther south. The largest concentration in the Western Hemisphere now nests on Florida beaches between Cape Canaveral and Sebastian Inlet. At the heart of that range is the Archie Carr National Wildlife Refuge. Every year 15,000 to 20,000 sea turtles—mostly loggerheads, but also a few dozen green turtles and leatherback turtles—nest on the refuge's 20.5 miles of sandy beach.

That moonlit night in August my family and I were visiting the Archie Carr Refuge in hopes of seeing just one nesting turtle. The odds were against us. The season was ending and only a few stragglers had been seen during the past few nights. Our guide, Joe Heeke, a volunteer naturalist for the Sea Turtle Preservation Society, warned us we might be disappointed.

But we were lucky. We came across tracks in the sand, a trail so prominent it was visible even in the weak light of the moon. On closer examination it looked as if it had been made by some clawing, dripping machine that had hauled itself from the ocean. Then we glanced up and saw, near the top of the beach, the shadowy shape of a turtle. In the moonlight it seemed as big as a capsized bathtub. About 300 pounds, said Joe. Middling-size.

A female sea turtle coming to the land from the water is alert and wary and can be turned back by a human voice or a bobbing flashlight. Once she begins digging her nest and laying her eggs, however, she becomes oblivious to the world. Even when harassed by coyotes and raccoons, robbed of her eggs as quickly as they are deposited, she will not be deterred from the job at hand.

Because we were a crowd—my wife and I, our two sons, my wife's parents, and Joe—we were concerned that our numbers might alarm the turtle. Joe told us not to worry. The people who do the harm, he said, are those who for some reason feel compelled to ride on the backs of the turtles. Our discreet observation was harmless.

Joe explained that location of the nest is critical. It must be placed above the reach of the tide, in sand that is not too wet and not too dry. If a nest is too close to the water, a storm surge can inundate it. If it is too high on the beach the hatchlings are more likely to become lost or captured by predators during their long dash to the water.

Using flippers the size of a first baseman's mitt to clear sand from the surface, the turtle had made a shallow body pit. When she reached sand of the proper temperature and moisture, she used alternating scoops of her rear flippers to excavate a flask-shaped egg cavity. It was one of the two to six clutches she probably laid that summer.

We watched the turtle deposit eggs, two or three at a time in quick succession, until about 100 filled the cavity. When she was finished, she disguised the nest site with broad, jerky sweeps of her flippers, filling the egg cavity and scattering damp sand across an area large enough to make it look like someone had buried a compact car. Exhausted, she lumbered down the beach to the water. A wave struck her but could not lift her bulk. She continued deeper into the water until she floated in backwash. Another wave came and she disappeared.

But while she was still on the beach, still laying eggs, my son Aaron gave a surprised jump where he sat in the sand. "Crab," he said, thinking a ghost crab had scuttled across his hand. We turned to look and beside him the sand was boiling with tiny loggerhead turtles. Dozens of them. They were emerging from a nest made some sixty days earlier by this or another mature turtle.

The hatchlings obviously knew what they had to do. With a single-mindedness born of thousands of generations of natural selection, they scurried speedily through the loose sand toward the water. As soon as they touched the surf, they began swimming frantically and disappeared with the receding backwash.

Until recently, the destination of those hatchlings remained one of the enduring mysteries of the seas. Biologists spoke of the early months of turtle life as the "lost year."

That mystery occupied famed biologist Archie Carr much of his career. In his 1967 book, *So Excellent A Fishe: A Natural History of Sea Turtles*, he wrote: "I have never been able to locate a place, or anybody who knew of a place, where little sea turtles of *any* kind could be caught. Not even one little sea turtle. I never even heard rumors of the existence of such a place..." Carr could think of only one area where the young turtles might be found: "That place is among the floating rafts of sargasso weed, which drift in tropical currents and accumulate in vast volume in the Sargasso Sea."

Not long before his death in 1987, Carr found proof that his hunch had been correct. He and his colleagues discovered large numbers of juvenile sea turtles living happily in the sargassum rafts of the mid-Atlantic. Or perhaps not so happily: They are often found suffocated in patches of waste oil or tangled in the debris that circles in the Sargasso Sea.

But another mystery endured. How could a turtle the size of a silver dollar find its way through strong ocean currents and hundreds of miles of open ocean to feeding grounds in the mid-Atlantic, then find its way back, ultimately to nest on the same beach where it was born?

In 1994, a plausible explanation was offered by marine biologist Kenneth Lohmann, of the University of North Carolina at Chapel Hill. Lohmann discovered that sea turtles are equipped with a sophisticated magnetic compass in their heads. They use the compass to tap into the earth's magnetic field, which makes it possible to tell one direction from another and to determine how far north or south they have traveled. With other navigational skills, including the sense of smell and the ability to take cues from wave motion and the direction of light on the water, they can navigate the open sea with superb accuracy.

The early life of loggerheads, then, probably goes something like this: After hatchlings scramble from their nests they run toward the ocean, attracted to the brightest point on the horizon, which on an undisturbed beach is the flash of breaking waves or the stars and moon reflecting on the surface of the sea. They enter the surf and swim directly into the waves, a tactic guaranteed to take them away from shore. During their journey down the beach and through the surf, the turtles' internal magnetic compasses are set to point them toward the open ocean. The turtles maintain this bearing during their first few days, when they are engaged in what is called a "swim frenzy," a period of virtually ceaseless swimming day and night that carries them into deep water. Throughout this frenzy, the hatchlings live off the reserves stored in their yolks. By the time their frenzied activity ends, the turtles have safely reached the Gulf Stream, which carries them north and east into the Sargasso Sea, where they find cover and an abundant supply of edible invertebrates among the floating sargassum weed. They probably remain there for several years, until late adolescence, when they set out for feeding grounds closer to shore. At sexual maturity, age twenty or thirty, the females return to the beaches of their birth to make nests of their own.

That night on the beach we witnessed two widely separated points on that enormous migratory circle. With the adult depositing eggs in the sand and the hatchlings clawing to the surface and running toward the water, we were in the midst of what was clearly the natural order of things. Once in the water the hatchlings would be targeted by sharks, mackerel, redfish, snook, snappers, and many other predators. Probably fewer than one out of a hundred would survive to adulthood.

I could not resist touching the adult turtle. Her shell was soft and studded with barnacles and strings of algae. I bent and sniffed her: a smell like deep forest spritzed with brine and musk. Then, as have many tourists before me, I reached beneath the turtle and caught a falling egg. It was wet and rubbery and tough, with the heft of a Ping-Pong ball filled with gelatin. I thought of the turtle that would hatch from it, the challenges it would face, the journey it would undergo. In the grand balance of nature that egg weighed tons.

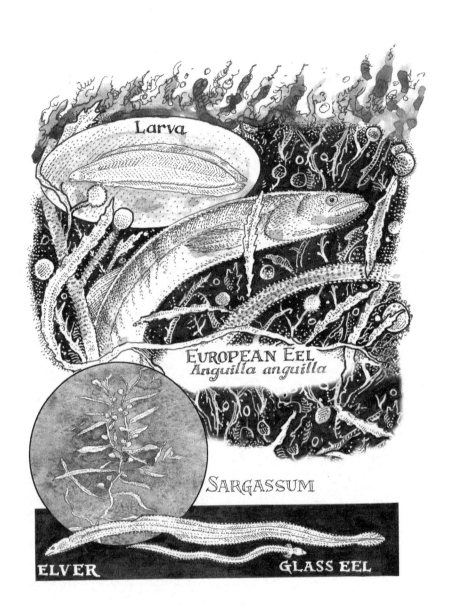

Larva

EUROPEAN EEL
Anguilla anguilla

SARGASSUM

ELVER GLASS EEL

16

WIDE SARGASSO SEA

The Sargasso Sea is unlike any sea on earth. It has no easily seen boundaries, no shores, none of the defining characteristics of the Mediterranean, North, Black, or Red. Yet for hundreds of years mariners have spoken of this sea in the midst of an ocean with fear and superstition. It is a place of weeds and bizarre creatures, of eerie windless silences and endless swells, where sailors driven to madness die and spend eternity trapped on ghost ships that go nowhere.

It is also a place where an assortment of well-adapted residents and migrants find habitat where there should be none. The Sargasso isn't quite teeming with life—many biologists have labeled it a biological desert— but plants and animals live there in concentrations sufficient to make it one of the most unusual ecosystems in all the oceans.

The absolute location of the Sargasso Sea varies. Oceanographers tend to limit it to a portion of the middle North Atlantic containing surface water that remains 64 degrees Fahrenheit year-round. Geologists define it by the ocean basin it covers. Biologists define it as the area where *Sargassum* weed is found. Generally speaking, it's at the center of the North Atlantic, circled by the immense current system known as the

North Atlantic current gyre. Approximately the size of the United States, it covers the deepest portion of the North Atlantic basin, and is bounded on the west by North America's continental shelf and on the east by the Mid-Atlantic Ridge. Only the Bermuda Islands break its surface. It was named centuries ago by the same Portuguese sailors who spread rumors of ships trapped in rafts of clinging weeds, in a region where no winds blew and the sea stank with corruption. Within the Sargasso, they said, damaged ships drifted aimlessly and crews grew crazed from lack of water and food. The rumors thrived, even after Columbus and his terrified crew sailed a course straight through the sea of weeds and came out the other side. Though most of the old legends of the Sargasso have disappeared, the myth of a "Bermuda Triangle" overlapping the Sargasso Sea has endured. Modern tales of aircraft and ships subject to bizarre phenomena and mysterious disappearances are echoes of the old Sargasso tales.

Oceanographers consider the Sargasso Sea the best example of *geostrophic flow*—the tendency for water at the center of circular ocean currents to be raised in a gently sloping mound about a meter above normal sea level. The mound is caused when a combination of wind-driven currents and the Coriolis force pile surface water in the center of a gyre. Gravity causes the water to flow in a definite but very slow current from the top of this mound outward.

The weed of the Sargasso is *Sargassum*, a large rootless alga kept on the surface by small translucent floats the Portuguese thought looked like "little grapes" and named accordingly. It is abundant in the Sargasso Sea, but not in quantities that could slow a passing boat. It collects in scattered flotillas, fewer in number now than in the days of early mariners, but probably never dense enough to match legendary reports. Until the voyage of the *Challenger* in 1872, it was assumed that sargassum weed was uprooted from coastal weed beds and carried into the Sargasso Sea where it remained trapped until it died. Scientists on the *Challenger*, however, discovered that the plant was pelagic: It lives, reproduces, and dies in the open sea.

Sargassum weed reproduces in a most practical way for an open-ocean plant. It is asexual, so it does not depend on chancy fertilization, and requires only that the tips of its branches occasionally break off, drift away, and develop into full-sized plants of their own. In time, as an individual plant ages, it produces fewer and fewer of the gas bladders that keep it afloat, and eventually it begins a slow descent into the abyss.

But while it lives, a sargassum plant is the whole world to many animals, from hydrozoans and bryozoans to polychaete worms, barnacles, crabs, shrimp, and young sea turtles. Finning among the branches of the plant are tiny fish—filefish, driftfish, pipefish, and the amazingly well-camouflaged sargassum fish, *Histrio histrio*, which looks like nothing as much as a hunk of sargassum with fins. So many organisms live in the rafts of weeds that their combined weight occasionally sinks them. Some species cling to the weed because it happens to be the handiest floating object in the area. Others, like the sargassum fish, have lived there for so long they have adapted camouflage and other defenses to match the weedy environment.

Two other inhabitants of the Sargasso Sea—during part of their lives at least—are American and European eels. For centuries the life cycle of the eels was a mystery. Nobody knew how they reproduced or where they went when they migrated down their resident rivers in autumn and disappeared into the ocean. Aristotle conjectured that they were a kind of serpent that generated spontaneously from the mud in rivers. Izaak Walton in 1653 reported another popular theory in *The Compleat Angler*: "And others say...Eels are bred of a particular dew, falling in the months of May or June on the banks of some particular ponds or rivers, apted by nature for that end; which in a few days are, by the sun's heat, turned into eels."

Naturalists eventually realized that the large dark eels of American and European rivers and the smaller, transparent eels known as glass eels or elvers that were sometimes found in estuaries were actually different stages in the life of the same creature. But not much else was known about them until 1920, when Danish oceanographer Johannes Schmidt discovered large numbers of tiny, transparent eel larvae drifting with other plankton among sargassum rafts in the Sargasso Sea. Schmidt concluded that the mature eels migrated to the Sargasso Sea, mated, spawned, and died, and that their larvae stayed in the Sargasso until eventually they rode the Gulf Stream back to coastal rivers where they matured.

But some mysteries endure. It's not known how the eels navigate during their journey from river to sea to river. And to this day nobody has found a mature eel in the Sargasso Sea.

17
RHAPSODY IN FEATHERS

The world has rarely known a person with more delicate sensibilities than Craig Date. One lovely June morning, I watched him crawl from his tent beside the Au Sable River, look up into trees alive with singing birds, and shout as loudly as he could, "Shut up!"

He was joking, of course. Nobody wants to silence the birds. But even if Craig had meant it, his shout would have made no impact. He was ignored, absolutely. The birds sang on in their business and pleasure, and no doubt they will sing as long as they live. May they flourish.

The singing of birds has always fascinated and delighted people. Caged songbirds were highly prized in ancient Greece and Rome, giving rise to thriving importation businesses. When Cortés sought revenge on the Aztec empire, he burned and leveled not only the temples of Tenochtitlan, but the vast aviary that was the pride of that great doomed city. Nature writers from Aristotle to Thoreau to Annie Dillard have sung the praises of bird songs, and innumerable ornithologists have made it their life's work. At least some of the influence of Rachel Carson's 1963 denunciation of the careless use of pesticides, *Silent Spring*, was due to the suggestion in her title that we might someday face a world without birdsong.

In past ages people were often tempted to believe that birds sing for the same reason humans do—for the joy of it, or to entertain people—but biologists long ago put those notions to rest. We now know that birds sing for two very good reasons: to attract mates and to define territories.

Observers have long noticed that in many parts of the world the most energetic singing occurs near sunrise, especially in spring and summer. This wild medley of clear, strong birdsong is called the dawn chorus and was once explained in strictly romantic terms as serenading lovers, or as mourners grieving lost mates, or as father birds celebrating the satisfactions of family life. The romantics had one detail correct: it is mostly male birds that sing, at least in the upper latitudes (in the tropics, males and females of many species engage in duets). Ornithologists now believe a combination of several theories explains the dawn chorus. One is that birds sing most vigorously at dawn because there are fewer noises with which to compete, thus increasing the chances that they'll be heard. Another is that dawn, with its poor light, is an unfavorable time to hunt or forage for food, so it might as well be put to other good use. A third is that at dawn a male bird can advertise himself as a desirable mate, one strong enough to survive the night and hearty enough to sing about it.

Why birds sing has sometimes been debated, but how they sing is well known. Songbirds are equipped with a vocal organ called a syrinx, named for the wood nymph Syrinx in Greek mythology, who escaped the lusty attentions of Pan by transforming into a marsh reed of the sort that can be fashioned into a musical pipe. The syrinx is located at the bottom of a bird's trachea, where it divides into two bronchi leading into the lungs. Within the syrinx are a number of membranes connected to muscles. When air from the lungs passes over the membranes they vibrate; tone and pitch are adjusted by the syringeal muscles. Songbirds are equipped with as many as nine pairs of muscles, accounting for their vocal virtuosity, while birds that sing little or merely grunt or squawk have few or no such muscles.

The syrinx is capable of producing sounds of great variety and subtlety.

Accomplished birders can identify hundreds of bird species by their songs, yet even the most gifted human ear has limitations. Sensitive devices, such as the sound spectrograph, have demonstrate that many songs are too complex for our narrow range of hearing to appreciate. We're deaf to many of the highest-pitched and most rapidly delivered notes.

What we can hear, however is amazing. Ornithologists have counted the musical outputs of certain birds and come up with astonishing figures. A red-eyed vireo was once observed singing a two-to-four-note song 22,197 times in one fourteen-hour period. A musical prodigy that is a particular favorite of mine and my wife's is the brown thrasher. This large mimid—a relative of the mockingbird and catbird—has the greatest repertoire of any North American songbird and has been credited with as many as 3,000 melodies. It likes to take up a position at the top of an aspen or birch in partially open terrain, where it can be seen and heard to full advantage, and deliver strings of jazzlike riffs mimicked from other birds and some of its own invention, delivering them with seemingly boundless energy. Once you hear the song you're not likely to forget it, but mnemonic help is available nonetheless. The early twentieth-century ornithologist and musician F. Schuyler Mathews noted that the brown thrasher's song offers useful words of advice to farmers: "Shuck it, shuck it; sow it, sow it; Plough it, plough it; hoe it, hoe it." Thoreau reported in Walden that the thrasher's "rigmarole, his amateur Paganini performances," kept farmers company as they planted corn with the constant reminder: "Drop it, drop it, —cover it up, cover it up,—pull it up, pull it up, pull it up."

Another virtuoso is the marsh warbler of Europe and Asia. This small and unassuming warbler spends only two months of the year in its breeding grounds from the British Isles to the Ural Mountains of Siberia, then migrates to tropical Africa—a round-trip of about 4,800 miles. During its migrations the marsh warbler hears a great variety of bird songs, which it faithfully incorporates into a repertoire it uses during three to four days of virtual nonstop singing each spring. A Belgian scientist who spent nearly ten years studying marsh warbler songs found that they mimicked more than 210 species of birds and averaged seventy-six different imitations during each thirty-minute burst of song.

It takes a better-trained ear than mine to decipher such complex variations. At least once each spring I'm brought up short by a lovely, lilting, and altogether unfamiliar song. "What is that?" I wonder. Then I realize it's a robin. I seem incapable of recognizing from year to year the robin's flexing intonations and I have not been able to successfully transpose them into an English rendition. The songs and calls of some birds are so obvious that the birds have been named for them—killdeer, chickadee, whippoorwill, chewink, and peewee come to mind—but there are innumerable possible renditions of other songs. To me the song of a white-throated sparrow sounds something like "Oh see see see, Oh see see see"; yet others claim they hear "Old Sam Peabody, Peabody, Peabody," or "All day whittlin,' whittlin,' whittlin,' " or "Sweet Canada, Canada, Canada."

Interpretation is in the ear of the beholder, certainly, but there are differences among birds as well. Every bird sings a slightly individualized song, its own vocal signature, which varies with its age and with how often it has been exposed to the songs of other birds. There are also dialects among songbirds of the same species. In one celebrated study, female European chiffchaffs were rigged with electrodes that measured their heart rates. When male chiffchaffs sang, the hearts of females from the same region beat up to 12 percent faster. But when males from other regions sang, the females did not respond at all.

We're a musical species ourselves and value melody enough to make distinctions between bird songs and bird calls. A song stirs something in the soul, while a call is mere utility. The songs of thrushes and nightingales inspire poetry, while the croak of a raven investigating roadkill or the single alarm note of a chickadee announcing the approach of a cat scarcely warrants mention. A song sparrow sings and is revered for it; a cowbird calls and F. Schuyler Mathews calls it a "disreputable character, parasitic in habit and degenerate in all moral instinct... his nearest approach to music is a sort of guttural murmuring... a harsh, metallic gluck, zee-zee without rhythm or sentiment. Why should they have either? The bird has no song—no mate to call. He is a polygamist, a bird of no principles, a 'low-down character.' He usually goes with a flock of other evil spirits just like himself…"

The catbird-hating Mathews was the author of one of the earliest and certainly the most unusual guides to bird-song, a 1910 volume titled, *Field Book of Wild Birds and Their Music*, with the weighty subtitle, *A Description of the Character and Music of Birds, Intended to Assist in the Identification of Species Common in the United States East of the Rocky Mountains*. Mathews was dissatisfied with conventional efforts to translate bird songs into human language—the example that most offended his ear was "Old Sam Peabody, Peabody, Peabody," for the white-throated sparrow—so he set out over a period of twenty years to transpose the songs of 126 North American bird species into musical scores. Those scores can be played on a piano, but Mathews insisted they should be whistled. But it was easier said than done. The songs he transposed included complex chords that required whistling two notes simultaneously and contained cascades of notes as dense as sixty-four to the bar.

Last spring Gail and I watched a Baltimore oriole singing for a mate from the top of a tree in our front yard. He went on day after day, beginning every morning shortly before dawn, when Lake Michigan was so calm a tossed stone might have cracked it like a mirror. We had not seen a female oriole all spring, and Gail, whose instinct for matchmaking extends even to the birds, began to worry that this tirelessly balladeering male was doomed to remain a bachelor. Then one morning as we were working in the garden we saw a pair of male and female orioles chasing each other through the trees, swooping above our heads, playing branch-tag in the same maple where an oriole's nest from the previous year hung abandoned like an empty lunch sack. We even witnessed a brief fluttering dalliance on a branch. Satisfied that all was well with the world, Gail went back to raking the garden.

But I stood transfixed and tried to imagine what it would be like to sing like a bird. It should be easy, I thought: Gulp air until your breast swells, tip your head back, open your mouth, and gush a river of melody. I cut loose, as loudly as I could, with the chorus of "Love is a Many Splendored Thing." Gail dropped her rake and covered her ears with her hands. The dog whined.

Suddenly, our lovesick orioles were nowhere to be seen, and not a single bird in the neighborhood was singing. It seemed I had silenced them all. My old friend Craig Date would have been mightily impressed.

18

THE MUSIC OF
THIS SPHERE

"The place is very well & quiet & the children only scream in a low voice."
—Lord Byron

My wife and I moved to the country in search of quiet, I think. It's hard to remember. Just before Christmas in 1991 we settled into a century-old farmhouse in a large yard filled with very large maples, in a neighborhood of meadows, orchards, and woodlots along the shore of Lake Michigan's Grand Traverse Bay. We brought our children, and the children, of course, brought their noise. Not much changed from our days in the Old Town neighborhood of small but clamorous Traverse City except that we had more snow to shovel in the winter and more lawn to mow in the summer, and the neighbors, we noticed, did their own yard work with farm tractors. Much of the time, Gail and I still had to shout to make ourselves heard.

Our first night in the new house, with the boys upstairs and asleep at last, Gail and I lay in the darkness in the unfamiliar bedroom and admitted that our hopes for a quiet new life were probably in vain. The wind was up, blowing from the big lake, vibrating the storm windows in their frames and making the house hum like a tuning fork. During the blaring distractions of daytime, while we unpacked and the kids were turned up to full volume, we had failed to notice that the furnace in the basement ignites with an alarming bang, followed seconds later by three more bangs, as if someone were hammering the ductwork with a mallet: BANG! ...Bang, Bang, BANG! I got up and investigated, but all was well with the rumbling old oil burner. On my way back to bed, I stopped in the kitchen for a drink of water and discovered that after a few hours of disuse the faucet turns on with a sputter, a hiss, and an explosion of spray, followed by a low intestinal groaning of pipes deep in the basement.

That night I had a realization: Silence might be the voice of eternity, but the temporal world makes itself known through noise. Not only is silence not golden, it is unnatural. Everyone knows that wind, surf, and the rusty-hinge cries of gulls harmonize, like members of the same family of instruments. But astronomers who aimed instruments at the sky discovered that the stars and planets hum with gonglike resonance and that the Big Bang still echoes across the universe. Noise is everywhere and relentless. The music of the spheres turns out to be a grand clamor.

The clamor is great also in the animal kingdom. During the first warmish evenings in April, while the ice is still shelved along the shore of Lake Michigan, the spring peepers begin calling from near the ponds in the woods across the road. These tiny tree-frogs, found in most parts of North America, are among the first amphibians to vocalize every year. Like many other frogs, they perform their calls in groups of three, forming a chorus. Typically, one initiates the performance by repeating a single note, an A. If there is no answer it sends out a high-pitched trill. A second frog adds a single answering note—a G-sharp—and when the first frog responds, they call in duet for a time. Often that will inspire a third frog to chime in with a series of B notes. The trio then begins calling in sequence—A, G-sharp, B—over and over, and loudly.

Loud volume is not unusual during mating season, when the males of many animal species are uninhibited promoters of their own vitality. If territory is intruded upon, the roar of an elephant seal, the bugle of an elk, and the bellow of a bull alligator serve as "ownership displays" to warn away rival males and avoid physical conflicts which might inflict injury.

Vocal displays also attract mates, as do a seemingly endless number of other ingenious aural tactics. Male songbirds sing their signature melodies to attract females and stake out territories against other males. Male grouse stand erect and beat their wings rapidly, compressing air into a surprisingly loud "drumming" that begins slowly and ends rapidly— about fifty beats in ten seconds. A woodpecker pecks a signature beat on a hollow tree or branch that is recognized by others of its species. In a tactic known as "winnowing," a Wilson's snipe dives from hundreds of feet in the air until it reaches a speed of twenty-four miles per hour, then spreads its tail feathers to make them vibrate so loudly the sound can be heard from a mile away. A male cicada attracts mates with a shrill buzzing call made by vibrating drum membranes over cavities on each side of its thorax. The clicker butterflies Charles Darwin observed in Brazil during his voyage on H.M.S. Beagle attract mates by popping their wings together with a sound like rapidly snapped fingers, or, as Darwin noted, "similar to that produced by a toothed wheel passing under a spring catch."

Mating calls go on even when an animal would be decidedly better off staying quiet. Ruffed grouse reduce the risk of advertising for a mate by drumming at sites surrounded by thick cover to protect them from owls and hawks. Frogs of Central and South America are preyed upon by bats that hunt them by listening to their calls and determining which frogs are edible and which are poisonous. The frogs are caught in a dilemma. If they stop calling they fail to mate, but if they call recklessly they die. The only solution is to be very alert and become instantly silent if they detect overhead motion or sound.

The cacophony does not end with mating season, of course. Within a caucus of crows you might hear calls of warning, which send all crows in the vicinity winging away to safety; calls of distress if a bird has been captured or injured; or assembly calls, which attract crows from all directions to mob a cat or hawk. The common (or Eurasian) blackbird gives at least two alarm calls: a drawn-out *seeeeee* when a predator is spotted flying overhead, and a repetitive *chuck-chuck-chuck* or *pook-pook-pook* when one is on the ground. A greater prairie chicken mother emits a low-pitched *brirrb-brirrb* call and her chicks come running, but when her call is high-pitched and shrill, the chicks freeze in place. Social animals use various vocalizations to signal alarm, warning, distress, or food, and to maintain and challenge the hierarchy of dominance within a group. Wolves may howl to assemble the members of a pack, to communicate with other packs, or even, in the words of one researcher, "for the heck of it."

In many parts of the world, nearly constant background music is made in summer by the scraper-and-file stridulations of crickets, grasshoppers, and katydids. These singing insects—or fiddling insects, since their music is never produced vocally—are highly expressive and surprisingly sophisticated. Songs have been identified as "common" (expressing, perhaps, nothing but well-being), "seeking" (performed by males trying to locate females), "rivalry" (between competing males), "disturbance" (caused by persistent rivals), "courting" (by males who have found females), and "reduced" (just before and during mating).

Animals that make warning sounds are seeking to avoid potentially injurious clashes. A dog growls, a cat hisses (which is effective, it's been theorized, because it imitates the hiss of a snake—an argument that has also been used to explain why a cat swings its tail back and forth), a scorpion squeaks as it arches it tail, and a rattlesnake activates its rattle with a sudden buzz. Many tropical geckos make loud clicking or squawking sounds and lunge at enemies to frighten them away. Crocodiles as well as many turtles and tortoises open their mouths wide and hiss in warning.

Nor is the noise limited only to the surface. When scientists submerged microphones in the oceans for the first time in the 1940s they were surprised to discover that the seas are not the silent world they assumed them to be. There's a tremendous range and variety of sounds going on underwater, at every depth and in every season. Among the most celebrated are the songs of the humpback whale, which last from six to thirty minutes each, are repeated for hours at a time, and can be heard by other humpbacks through many miles of water. But even the vocalizations of much smaller marine animals have surprised researchers. Many fish, for instance, produce complex sounds. Researchers at the Narragansett Marine Laboratory in the 1950s identified calls among many fish that communicated "aggravation, alarm, and readiness for combat." Other vocalizations are used to attract mates, to keep fish close to one another in schools, and to define and defend territories. Some fish are so noisy—toadfish, drums, grunts, and croakers come to mind—that they are named for the sounds they make when they strike hollow swim bladders with special drumming muscles along their backbones.

Marine catfish bark, sea horses click, and codfish grunt. Sea bass beat their gill covers against their heads. Triggerfish, ocean sunfish, horse mackerel, and squirrelfish make rasping sounds by grinding together special teeth located in their throats. Male satinfish shiners purr to attract females. A male toadfish looking for a mate roars with a sound like a foghorn, then growls while guarding the eggs he has fertilized.

Many marine crustaceans send auditory signals to establish territories, attract mates, or warn of danger. Spiny lobsters repel intruders with a scratching sound made by rubbing the base of their claws when a predator comes near, causing every crab in the vicinity to seek cover. Some of the loudest inhabitants of the oceans, the Alpheidae family of shrimp known as snapping shrimp or pistol shrimp, are small, only two inches long, but they make a very big noise. They can snap their claws to produce retorts as loud as firecrackers that shoot a "bubble bullet" at more than seventy miles per hour through the water. The blast is powerful enough to stun prey and repel predators.

With so much noise going on in the world, surely it's a mistake to think that children should be seen and not heard. My wife and I knew all along that our kids would not run shouting through the house forever. They would grow and move their noisy selves elsewhere and only on weekends and holidays would the house be filled again with their laughter and conversation. If they should have children of their own someday it will be our duty to set them loose in the house with battery-powered fire trucks and drum sets and other toys that employ clappers, bells, gongs, and whistles.

What if the record of our lives is kept in a kind of musical score, every spoken word a note, every passionate speech a bravura, every stomp of foot and clap of hand a ringing counterpoint? Maybe, in our final moments, the entire score is played back for us and we recognize where we should have added volume, where we should have given the brass section freedom, where we should have pounded chords with abandon.

There is plenty of noise in a house with children, and with Aaron and Nick grown and on their own, I admit I miss it. I miss the footsteps pounding down the hallway, each boy bracketed in his zone of commotion. They run to their bedroom, slam the door, and start whacking tennis balls against the walls with hockey sticks. It's the sound of well-being. Every parent dreads the silent pauses. They mean injury or misbehavior, a toddler drawing that long breath before a bawl of pain, a four-year-old lugging the puppy to the toilet for a bath.

If silence is an unnatural state in the universe, children are only doing what comes naturally. And who are we to tamper with nature? I say kids should hoot and holler, wail and whistle, bang, clang, stomp, and clatter. They should run through the house with gusto. They should exult. They should be jubilant. They should shout and be heard. The noise of my sons in action has always been music to my ears. It's as soothing to me as birdsong.

(Parthenogenic) NEW MEXICAN WHIPTAIL

DRONE

QUEEN

ANGLERFISH

CLEANER WRASSE

19
WEIRD SEX

Life on our planet is so diverse it's a wonder that we aren't more tolerant of diversity in all its forms. Take sex, for instance. Most living things pursue the business of reproduction so earnestly that witnessing a little foreplay on television or in the behavior of a young couple in the back of a public bus seems—to me, at least—a very small matter. Not everyone agrees, of course. A friend of mine once tried to divert her impressionable young daughter's attention from a sudden love scene on television by shouting, "Quick! Look outside!" then turned with her in time to see, through the front window, a pair of dogs copulating in their yard. Birds do it, bees do it, even neighborhood mongrels do it. It's probably time we got used to the idea.

Our interest in sex is apparently limitless, though it tends to follow predictable pathways. We are naturally most interested in human sex—that assortment of awkward couplings that has been the source of so much celebration and ridicule through the ages—which is undoubtedly why we spend so little time considering options other than the heterosexual and homosexual varieties most of us are familiar with. But there are other possibilities to consider.

Science-fiction writers seem to be more aware of that than the majority of people. The figments of their randy imaginations could fill a bizarre and mildly pornographic encyclopedia of sex on other worlds. But for every Ixtl from the planet Glor (which reproduces, says A.E. van Vogt, by implanting an indestructible egg in the body of a living host, in the manner of Sigourney Weaver's archenemy in *Alien*) and every mating pair of Polarians (which, according to Piers Anthony, ambulate on ball bearings instead of legs and mate by spinning together in dizzying circles until, in a frenzy, they swap ball bearings), there is a land snail or deep-sea anglerfish here on Earth that makes the mating of extraterrestrials seem dull and chaste by comparison. The ocean depths and terrestrial crannies of this fertile world are steaming with innovative reproductive antics. Love may make the world go round but weird sex keeps it populated.

Considering how important sex is to humans, it might be surprising to note that among many animals, sex is not only overrated, it's unnecessary. In 1958 a Russian biologist named Ilya Darevsky created a stir when he announced that some populations of small lizards of the genus *Lacerta* were composed only of females, and that those females were able to reproduce perfectly well without any assistance from males. This process, call parthenogenesis—the development of an individual from an egg that has not been fertilized—results in cloned offspring that are genetically identical to their mothers. Such virgin births are not limited to *Lacerta* lizards. About a thousand species of animals do it, including several whiptail lizards found in the southwestern United States and quite a few flatworms, leeches, and scale insects.

Parthenogenesis might be an inspiration to countless women grown weary of the males in their lives, but it has a basic problem. Sexual reproduction mixes male and female genes, resulting in offspring that are genetically variable and thus more adaptable than the identical clones of parthenogenesis. To get some genetic mixing, many of the animals that reproduce parthenogenetically will also reproduce sexually when males are available. Gall wasps, for example, reproduce in alternating generations. One generation, made up of both males and females, will mate and produce only females. Those females then reproduce parthenogenetically and give birth to a generation of mixed genders.

Among the social bees, sex is determined by a variation known as optional parthenogenesis, in which the queen, who mates only once in her life and stores male sperm in a sperm sac, gives birth to fertilized and unfertilized eggs. The fertilized eggs always hatch into females that become either fertile queens or sterile workers, while the unfertilized eggs hatch into males whose only purpose is to fertilize future queens.

A kind of parthenogenesis is practiced by a small, stream-dwelling fish of Texas and Mexico known appropriately enough as the Amazon molly. All Amazon mollies are females, yet their eggs require male sperm to stimulate development, a condition that forces the mollies to solicit males of other species within the genus for assistance. Once the sperm from another species comes in contact with the eggs of an Amazon molly, the eggs begin to develop, but without any of the chromosomes from the unwitting gigolo.

Fans of the original *Star Trek* television series might remember a classic episode, "The Trouble with Tribbles," in which the crew of the *Enterprise* is introduced to small, cute, furry creatures that turn out to employ an unusual reproductive system. Tribbles have the ability to be born already pregnant. Thus they are able to reproduce at warp speed, and in almost no time at all the *Enterprise* is filled to bursting with the huggable critters.

A similar strategy for explosive reproduction is used by a tiny insect that infests many garden and house plants: the aphid. Aphids cluster in plump and defenseless bunches on twigs and leaves and are easy prey for insects, spiders, birds, and other predators. To survive they need a reproductive strategy that is quick and foolproof and allows them to take advantage of temporarily abundant food, colonize new plants when necessary, and be free of the time-consuming work of finding mates, courting, and mating. In spring a wingless female aphid hatches from an egg laid the previous year near the bud of a plant, say a rose. She promptly drills her snout into the rosebud and begins sucking its sap. Within a few days or weeks she gives birth, one after another, to live, identical, female offspring. She might have twenty-five daughters a day, and each of her daughters gives birth to twenty-five daughters of her own every day. The population expands exponentially—an entomologist once calculated that a single aphid under ideal conditions (with no predators or diseases to contend with) could produce 600 million descendants in a single year. When the rose can support no additional aphids, a generation of females is born with wings and they fly off to find fresh plants upon which to establish their own female dynasties.

Males aren't needed until the end of summer, when tender plants become scarce. At that time, the year's final generation of parthenogenic females gives birth to both males and females. They mate and the females lay their eggs in prime spots on roses and other plants where they remain dormant until the next spring.

*

Most animals that reproduce sexually can be identified as either males or females, but not all of them consider the differences significant. Most slugs and many land snails are hermaphrodites, with each individual being both male and female. They mate by selecting a member of their own species that matches the complex shape of its sex organs and exchanging sperm simultaneously. Caribbean sea bass of the genus *Hypoplectrus* are also hermaphrodites. They mate in pairs and take turn releasing eggs and sperm into the water.

It's sometimes easier to change sexes than to wait for a mate of the opposite sex to appear. That's the case with a number of reef fishes, including the cleaner wrasse of Australia's Great Barrier Reef. Typically, a male cleaner wrasse will claim and defend a section of reef for himself, then gather a harem of about a half dozen smaller females. If the male dies, however, the largest female in the harem undergoes a sex change. Within a few days she transforms into a male and mates successfully with the females in the harem.

Where mates are scarce, bizarre adaptations often arise. Perhaps the most bizarre of all occurs among several species of anglerfish that live in the deepest, darkest, and least inhabited portions of the Atlantic and Antarctic oceans. The female anglerfish is large, up to three feet in length, with enormous jaws and formidable teeth and a thin appendage resembling a fishing rod that juts from her dorsal fin and dangles a bioluminescent "bait" in front of her mouth, where it blinks to attract prey. The male is so different in appearance that it was once classified as a separate species. He is small and unremarkable and starts life as a resident of surface waters. At maturity, however, he descends to deep water in search of a female. But because mates are so scarce in the abyssal depths, once he finds a female he attaches himself to her with his teeth and with a special bone on the first spine of his dorsal fin, clamping her so securely that the connection between them becomes permanent. In time, the body of the female grows over the head of the male, they merge circulatory systems, and the male loses all his internal organs except his testes and becomes entirely dependent upon the female for food and oxygen. In this way a female can collect and carry six or more males on her body. When she is ready to spawn, she signals the males with hormones and they release clouds of sperm to fertilize her eggs.

It's difficult not to be horrified by the sex lives of bedbugs. The male of these parasites is equipped with a sharp, swordlike penis with which he practices what biologists call "traumatic copulation," but which any jury would call rape. After sneaking up on a female he stabs her with his penis, piercing her abdomen, then deposits sperm in her hemocoel, the body cavity through which all her blood passes. The sperm finds its way to the female's heart and is pumped to her reproductive tract. In the case of the African bedbug, *Xylocaria maculipennis,* the male bedbug's copulation is not limited to females. In what is apparently an effort to maximize his genetic potential, he will sometimes stab other males and inject sperm into them. When the victimized males perform their own rape of females, some of the first male's sperm is passed on as well.

Such assaults are not as deplorable as they seem. Bedbug sperm contains a great deal of protein, so the recipient gains nutritionally from insemination. The benefits are attractive enough to have caused male *Afrocimex* bedbugs to mimic the appearance of females. According to biologist Adrian Forsyth in *A Natural History of the Sex*, these "transvestites" stimulate other males to inseminate them, either for the free protein or to deplete the sperm supply of rival males and increase their own chances of impregnating females.

All of which makes the birds and the bees a most complicated issue. Parents who dread The Big Questions About Life know that the biggest questions, the most difficult ones to answer to a child's satisfaction, are about sex. In compensation we tend to over-prepare.

That friend of mine whose daughter witnessed a pair of dogs copulating in the yard likes to tell another story about her misadventures in sex-ed. When her daughter was five years old, she asked, "Mommy, how do you make a baby?" The question came sooner than my friend expected, but she was ready. She took a deep breath and began. As she talked, she discovered that many of her explanations needed explanations, so she had to go into even more detail than she had planned. She discussed the reproductive strategies of dogs, birds, and people. She talked about the significance of the love in lovemaking. She gave concise, age-specific treatises on menstruation, birth control, and safe sex. When she finally finished, she noticed that her daughter had become agitated. She noticed also the crayons and drawing paper in her hands. "Mommy," the little girl said, almost in tears, "All I wanted to know is *how to make a baby.*"

20
ANIMAL DADS

Fatherhood did not come naturally to me. I seem to have inherited my own father's aversion to dirty diapers and regurgitated milk and the ability to sleep through the night while the baby cries. I always assumed I would be content to spend my days earning money and fixing broken stuff around the house, and my evenings stretched out on the couch watching ballgames. It took a good woman, better instructed than I in the ways of nature, to bring me to my senses.

No doubt many men would admit that the ideal male role is something like that of a lion. The king of beasts tends to be a lazy, self-indulgent brute that prefers to hang around with other males, has little patience with cubs, and spends as much as twenty-two hours a day sleeping while the females of the pride nurse and instruct the youngsters and haul home most of the food. The male's primary obligations are to defend the pride from attackers and to mate with the females of his choice. Not a bad life.

Yet, even the male lion occasionally grooms and plays with his offspring and other offspring within the pride. The truth is, gender roles that generations of humans once assumed were biologically mandated are not at all clear. In the animal kingdom, the male's role is often enough not very certain.

Birds are among the most diligent animal parents, the males and females of many species working in tandem to build nests, incubate eggs, and protect and feed offspring that require up to their own body weight in nutrients every day. Altricial young, those born naked and helpless, require so much attention it might be impossible for a single parent to raise them. A pair of adult house wrens were once observed making a total of 491 trips to their nest in a single day to feed their chicks. Species that nest in the Arctic often rest only during the one or two hours of twilight each night, devoting the daylight hours—twenty-two or twenty-three of them every day—to the rigors of parenthood.

In a number of bird species, the male takes a prominant parenting role. The male emperor penguin of Antarctica, for instance, incubates the single egg laid by his mate by balancing it on his feet and covering it with a fold of skin to keep it warm. During the two-month incubation, the female is at sea feeding and the male eats nothing, living off stored fat reserves and huddling for warmth with other incubating males. If the female has not yet returned by the time the egg hatches, the male will feed the hatchling during its first few days with a special secretion from his esophagus. After the female returns, both parents take turns waddling to the ocean for food and returning to supply their young penguin with a diet of regurgitated fish.

One of the hardest-working bird dads is the Namaqua sandgrouse of Africa's Kalahari Desert. Each day the male of a nesting pair flies as far as fifty miles to the nearest waterhole, where he soaks his belly feathers in water, then flies back to the nest, where the nestlings suck the water from his feathers. Although more than half the moisture may evaporate before he reaches the nest, his offspring manage to slake their thirst with about half an ounce of water each trip.

After the female silvery-cheeked hornbill of Africa selects a hollow in a tree as a nest site, the male helps her close the entrance with mud to protect her from predators. He then keeps his mate and the hatchlings fed through a small opening in the protective covering.

Some male birds take fatherhood a step further and do virtually all the raising of the young. In a mating system called polyandry, meaning "many males," which is found mostly among shore birds such as the spotted sandpiper, which breeds across North America and winters in Central and South America, and the northern jacana of coastal Mexico and Cuba, the females mate with several males, producing clutches with each of them, then abandon the nests, leaving the males to incubate the eggs and feed the chicks. In every regard except the actual development and laying of eggs, a polyandrous female exhibits characteristics that in most species are found in males. She is larger and more colorful than the male of her species—a reversal that caused Audubon and other early naturalists to misidentify the sexes of specimens they collected and painted—and she engages in elaborate attraction displays during the mating season.

Polyandry is rare among mammals. It is practiced occasionally by the marmoset, that tiny primate of Central and South America, along with monogamy and polygyny (in which the male mates with several females). In what is surely news to many, the mammal that practices polyandry most commonly is the human. In 2012 a team of anthropologists reported in the journal *Human Nature* that many societies across the globe and throughout history have considered it acceptable for a woman to marry or mate with more than one male partner at a time and for all the male partners to assist in raising the children. Those societies include about two dozen along the Tibetan plateau and another fifty-three elsewhere in the world.

But except for those relatively rare exceptions, in most mammal societies the female mates with a single male and becomes the primary caretaker of the young. Among the bears, for example, a nursing mother provides so well for her cubs that the father is unnecessary and abandons the family group. Typically, an adult male bear is gone long before the cubs he sired are born.

Many other male mammals play an active and important role in parenting. Males of pack-hunting canids—especially wolves, coyotes, jackals, and African wild dogs—often take responsibility for the feeding and care of pups. In a hierarchical social arrangement like that of the wolf, only the dominant male and female breed each year and their offspring become the responsibility of the entire pack. A lactating female is often brought food by her mate and other members of the pack. And the pups, once weaned, can usually depend on any adult of the pack to provide them with a freshly regurgitated meal, simply by whining and yelping and licking the adult's muzzle.

Among the primates, the male marmosets and tamarins of the rainforests of Central and South America are exceptionally devoted fathers and routinely look after the young. The male often carries his offspring, allowing them to cling to the fur of his back or belly. When an infant needs to feed, the male hands it to his mate, who suckles it. When she is finished, the male takes the infant again. He often offers morsels of food—fruit, saps and gums, frogs, lizards, and insects—to his nursing mate as well as to the youngsters.

Devoted dads can be found elsewhere in the animal kingdom, as well. The male midwife toad of Europe and northwestern Africa, after mating with a female, carries strings of fertilized eggs wrapped around his hind legs. For three weeks, he rests in his burrow by day, feeds at night, and when the eggs are in need of moisture, carries them to water for brief immersions. When the eggs are ready to hatch, he immerses himself in the water so the tadpoles can work free of the jelly around the eggs and swim away.

The mouth-breeding frog of Argentina, also known as Darwin's frog, employs a highly unusual reproductive strategy. For the first ten or twenty days after the female lays her eggs, the male stands guard over them. When they are nearly ready to hatch he picks the eggs up with his tongue and deposits them through slits in the bottom of his mouth into his swollen vocal sac. Safely inside, the eggs (as many as seventeen of them) continue to develop until they hatch into tadpoles. When the tadpoles are about half an inch long and their tails have disappeared, they climb from the vocal sac and leave their father's mouth.

The male green and black poison dart frog of Central and South America accepts the burden of fatherhood squarely on his shoulders. He mates with a female, who deposits her clutch of three to thirteen eggs in leaf litter and moves on. The male tends the eggs until they hatch, then encourages the tadpoles to wriggle up onto his back, where he holds them in place with a sticky mucus secretion, and carries them to any nearby pool of stagnant water, either on the ground or in a cavity in a tree or in the leaves of a bromeliad. When the tadpoles are ready to set off on their own, the father lowers himself into the water and they swim off.

The seahorse, certainly one of the oddest creatures in the sea, has evolved an unusual birthing mechanism that depends heavily on dad. When a male and female mate, the female deposits her eggs in a pouch on the belly of the male, where they are fertilized and remain until they hatch. Eventually the miniature seahorses, well fed on nutrients within the lining of their father's pouch, are expelled, and promptly swim off to begin an independent life.

Parenthood is a complex and highly variable skill, differing between individuals of a species as well as from species to species. George Schaller noted in his landmark study, *The Serengeti Lion*, that some female lions are dreadful mothers while others are very successful at the job. It's true as well of dads. Certain male chimpanzees and gorillas exhibit strong nurturing urges, while others are indifferent or even antagonistic to their offspring.

The same, of course, can be said of humans. Margaret Mead, in *Male and Female*, wrote that "human fatherhood is a social invention....Men have to learn to want to provide for others, and this behavior, being learned, is rather fragile and can disappear rather easily under social conditions that no longer teach it effectively."

Those of us who have been exposed to active fatherhood, who have entered the forbidding world of messy diapers and 3:00 a.m. feedings, would have it no other way. Like robins and wolves, we work better in tandem with our mates. Sure, we're brutes—clumsy, selfish, insensitive, reluctant to discuss our feelings—but we're transformed into absolute pussycats by a three-year-old climbing into our lap, nestling there, and saying with an upturned cherub's smile, "Daddy, I love you." We self-indulgent lions are suddenly eager to sacrifice our independence, youth, and expendable income to be the best of all possible dads.

21
MATES FOR LIFE

In spring a young man's fancy turns to love, and those friends of mine who are fathers of teenaged daughters could not be more miserable. They've grown vigilant, those nervous dads, peeking around their living-room drapes and complaining about the boys idling in cars at the curb and riding past on motorcycles, one wheel in the air and one eye on the house, and phoning, texting, and messaging on every available device. I remind my friends that humans sometimes mate for life, and that such long-term investments demand elaborate courtship rituals. They respond by saying that I, the father of boys, don't understand. Maybe. But I know from my own memories of courtship what a wonderful and terrible business it is. I suspect, in fact, that remembering the pain of courtship helps us to stay with the partner we choose.

It's encouraging that people across much of the world are quite successful at keeping their partners. The latest news from the marriage wars here in the United States is heartening: after sinking to a low in 1979, when 40 percent of the weddings performed in the United States were destined to end in divorce, successful marriages have been on the upswing. The divorce rate, which was at 5.3 per thousand people in 1981, fell to 3.6 per thousand in 2011. We're getting better at staying married.

That's a bit surprising to sociologists who predicted that divorces would continue to increase as generations of young people whose parents were divorced reached marrying age themselves. Many of us were ready to agree with the curmudgeonly British philosopher Bertrand Russell, who once declared, "Even in civilized mankind faint traces of monogamous instinct can be perceived."

Those of us determined to keep those faint traces from getting fainter are in both smaller and larger company than we might imagine. Smaller because one survey of human cultures around the globe found that of 849 societies only 141 were truly monogamous; and larger because in the rest of the animal kingdom a surprising number of species have found it an advantage to maintain sexual relationships with one partner.

About 90 percent of the world's 8,800 or so bird species practice one form or another of monogamy. Most, like the Eastern bluebird, are seasonally monogamous, courting a new mate each breeding season and staying together until their offspring are fledged. Other species change mates several times in a season, raising a brood with each. Still others are fairly faithful, the male establishing a monogamous relationship but occasionally indulging in extra-pair copulations.

A few birds are permanently monogamous, forming the kinds of long-term attachments many humans would envy. Canada geese sometimes become "engaged" up to a year before they reach breeding age, forming a pair bond that may last their entire lives. Cranes are so diligent in their monogamy that in Japan the red-crowned crane is considered a symbol of happy marriage. Most ravens and other corvids, as well as storks, swans, and some owls likewise form long monogamous relationships.

There is a simple reason why so many birds remain with one mate: the kids. The demands of raising young often take the full attention of two adults. Biologists like to discuss the behavior in economic terms, speaking of parental "investment," and pointing out that it is more profitable for a male bird intent on propagating his own genes to stick with one mate and ensure the survival of a brood than to impregnate many females haphazardly. Once committed to monogamy, a male bird takes the job seriously. He may help build nests, take turns brooding the eggs, gather food, and stand watch. In studies where the male has been removed, the numbers of eggs that hatch and fledglings that survive decline dramatically.

Species that stay together season after season may do so because it is energy efficient. Large birds exert so much energy in flight, especially during migration to summer nesting areas, that they have little to spare for the flashy and frivolous courtship games of smaller birds. A pair of Canada geese get right to the business of mating, nesting, and laying eggs, taking advantage of good weather and abundant food while they last, and giving their offspring a better chance to fledge and mature in time for the fall migration.

But what if you find that you can't live with your mate? Not all gulls mate for life, but among those that do there can be a biological mandate for divorce. Biologist William Jordan reports in his book, *Divorce Among the Gulls*, that more than 25 percent of newly paired gulls separate after the first attempt to raise young. They break up for some of the same reasons humans do, primarily good old-fashioned incompatibility. When a male and female gull are incompatible—say they both insist on doing all the brooding—they can spend so much time squabbling over who gets to sit on the nest that the eggs are forgotten. Gulls that fail to nest successfully usually divorce and return to the nesting area the following year with a different mate. Those that get along—and reproduce successfully—stay together.

Monogamy is much less common among mammals than birds. About 97 percent of mammal species are polygamous, the males mating with numerous females in an effort to maximize their genetic investments. Where bonding is more permanent, it is because it is more efficient genetically to stay with a female and help protect and feed the offspring. Foxes, wolves, and other canids stay together because they must cover a lot of territory to find food, and because a lactating female alone would have little hope of feeding and defending her young. Jackals in the Serengeti live in close-knit families composed of a monogamous male and female along with various young, including one or more adult offspring that assist in caring for their younger siblings. The klipspringer, a small African antelope, forms permanent pair bonds so that one mate can constantly watch for predators while the other grazes. Another African mammal, the tiny elephant-shrew, apparently bonds for life, but the male plays little part in rearing offspring and the bond is probably more useful in guarding the home range than in rearing young. Beavers expend a great deal of effort maintaining a lodge and cutting and storing a winter's supply of food. For many animals, it is more efficient to stay together than to wander promiscuously from mate to mate.

*

My wife tells me, in no uncertain terms, that I can be replaced. Hers is a biologically sound stance: most monogamous animals find another mate soon after the first one dies or is kicked out. But in countless animal stories from ancient times to the present, an animal that mates for life is committed. The factually unreliable but morally stout medieval bestiaries proposed that brides learn about marital fidelity from a turtle dove, which, when widowed, refuses to remarry, won't "break the bonds of chastity," and never "forgets the rights of her wedded husband."

In the late nineteenth and early twentieth centuries, nature writers like Ernest Thompson Seton became popular for their stories that were equally loaded with moral significance. Seton was successful from the moment his first book, *Wild Animals I Have Known*, was published in 1898, largely, one suspects, because of the sentimental appeal of his suspiciously human-like animals. Among the most beloved of his animal-heroes was the wolf Lobo, who died of a broken heart after the death of his mate Blanca. Seton's anthropomorphic portrayal of animals so repulsed John Burroughs that he initiated a famous feud by accusing Seton and writers like him of being "Nature Fakers."

Yet more than one reputable biologist has remarked on real incidents of animal grieving. Aldo Leopold noticed the lone geese that sometimes returned to his farm in March and decided they were "bereaved survivors of the winter's shooting, searching in vain for their kin." Mark Jerome Walters reports in his study of animal sexuality, *Courtship in the Animal Kingdom*, that the ornithologist George Archibald once watched a sandhill crane spend an entire summer lingering near a section of road outside Baraboo, Wisconsin. "It stood there like a gray ghost," Archibald said, "from dawn to dusk, every day from June till October. A state trooper told me its mate had been struck and killed by a car as the pair crossed the road. But their bond was so strong that when the female died, her mate returned to the same place every day, hoping that if he just waited long enough she would eventually come back to life."

*

Last spring my unmarried friends reported that the singles scene in that pheromone-laced season was only slightly less desperate than usual. Everybody was a little frisky and more inclined to be pleasant after the first date. There was an aura of impending urgency, as when the participants in a game of musical chairs sense the music will soon and abruptly end. No one wants to be left standing alone. But neither does anyone want to plop down in an ill-fitting chair.

We ought to know a thing or two about the courtship rituals of humans, but it's surprising how mysterious they remain. I've been married to the same fine woman for many years and I'm still not sure why our marriage works while so many in our generation have failed. Most years we celebrate our anniversary by booking a room or cabin in a region where there are migrating warblers and raptors to observe. We spend the day birding, hiking, or walking the beach, and in the evening go to a restaurant for a nice dinner. At some point, usually over the second glass of wine, we'll lean close and discuss the dynamics of long-term pair bonding. And that's when the sparks really start to fly.

PART III

THE SENSES

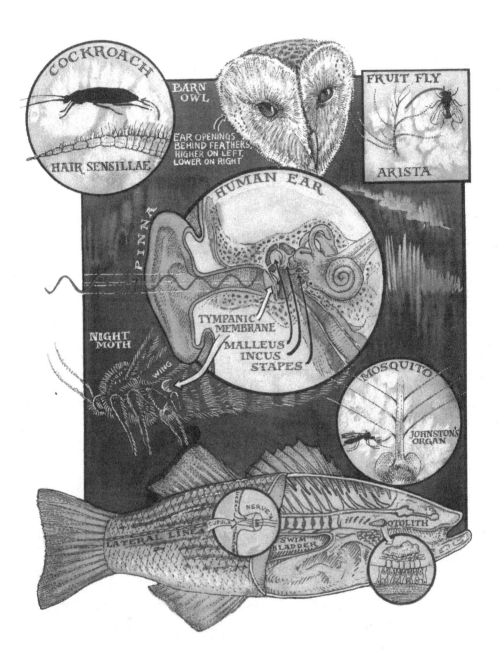

COCKROACH

HAIR SENSILLAE

BARN OWL

EAR OPENINGS
BEHIND FEATHERS,
HIGHER ON LEFT,
LOWER ON RIGHT

FRUIT FLY

ARISTA

HUMAN EAR

PINNA

TYMPANIC MEMBRANE

MALLEUS
INCUS
STAPES

NIGHT MOTH

WING

MOSQUITO

JOHNSTON'S ORGAN

NERVE

CUPULA

LATERAL LINE

SWIM BLADDER

OTOLITH

22
MY, WHAT BIG EARS YOU HAVE

My friends are starting to lose their hearing. They won't admit it, but surely it is because of those Led Zeppelin and Grateful Dead concerts in their youth. When my son was a teenager, he and I attended a Pearl Jam concert where we had front-row seats, facing speakers the size of compact cars. The volume didn't seem to bother Aaron, but I probably would have suffered permanent damage if a thoughtful security guard hadn't offered me his extra pair of ear plugs. He and I spent most of the evening catching kids as they fell from the edge of the mosh pit and trying to keep track of Aaron, who was in the middle of things, passing bodies over his head. The guard and I communicated with hand signals and by the end of the evening seemed like old friends. My ears rang for two weeks.

The point is, my father was right when he warned me all those years ago that listening to "Houses of the Holy" cranked up to unholy volume was bad for my ears. Hearing is a fairly fragile sense and, like all our senses, easy to take for granted until it begins to deteriorate. Loud music and other traumas can cause a pretty fast decline. When

I mention this to my gray-haired friends, they cock their heads, cup their ears, and say, "What?"

One of the ways we know the world is through the sounds it makes. Sound occurs when a moving or vibrating object creates a mechanical disturbance in air, liquid, or solid. A simple sound produces minor, predictable changes in atmospheric pressure. Those changes have troughs and peaks like waves in water and are transferred across space in undulations. Molecules in the air swing in a pendulum motion as the waves pass through them, becoming compressed at the peak of each wave and spreading out in each trough. The molecules themselves do not travel, but when they swing, they pass that to-and-fro motion to the molecules beside them. William Stebbins writes in *The Acoustic Sense of Animals*, that the motion is like a baton being passed "from runner to runner in a relay race."

As sound waves pass by, we reach out and grab a few and make guesses about their origins. Our ears are equipped to hear even slight variations in sound and our brains can sort them out, identify them, and signal thousands of responses. The system is sensitive enough to detect very subtle differences in wavelength, amplitude, timbre, and phase, making it possible for us to distinguish between a ringing phone and a ringing alarm clock, between the song of a rose-breasted grosbeak and that of a Baltimore oriole, between the words *run* and *rum* and *ear* and *hear*. Our ears are so central to our experiences and so finely tuned that we can even put them to work just for the pleasure of it. It's why we listen to Mozart and why we enjoy the sounds of ocean surf.

Humans don't have the best ears in the animal kingdom—far from it—but we're capable of hearing a pretty wide range of sounds. A standard measure of sound is its frequency in hertz, the number of sound waves per second. Human ears can detect frequencies as low as ten hertz (or ten vibrations per second) and as high as 20,000 hertz (20,000 vibrations per second). Sounds lower than ten hertz are known as infrasound; those higher are called ultrasound. Elephants can hear in a range from one hertz to 20,000 hertz. A dog whistle emits ultrasound at about 40,000 hertz, which is audible to a dog but not to us. Cats can hear frequencies as high as 70,000 hertz, but will respond to no whistle because, after all, they are cats. The champions of ultrasound are insect-eating bats capable of detecting frequencies of about 200,000 hertz. At the other end of the spectrum, some species of birds can hear infrasound frequencies as low as 0.1 hertz (or one vibration every ten seconds).

All ears work on a few basic principles. They convert sound waves to nerve impulses and transmit them to the brain for sorting and interpreting. The simplest systems, found in some cockroaches, grasshoppers, and caterpillars, accomplish this with organs known as hair sensillae. These free-moving hairs are hinged where they attach to the insect and respond to stimuli such as wind and low-frequency sound waves. More complex sound receptors include Johnston's organ, found at the base of a mosquito's antenna, and the featherlike arista of fruit flies. Both of these organs are stimulated when hairs on the antennae vibrate in response to certain sound frequencies.

The insects with the most highly developed hearing are probably crickets, locusts, cicadas, katydids, butterflies, and moths, all of which make use of tympanic membranes similar to the eardrums of land vertebrates. Their membranes are paired, usually one on each side of the body, and composed of a thin, taut section of exocuticle covering a cavity. The night moth has a pair of clefts, one beneath each wing, leading to tympanic membranes attached to receptor cells. The small oval ear openings of katydids are located below the knees on their front legs.

Fishes use two types of receptor systems. The most obvious are the lateral line canals along their flanks. They are comprised of tiny tentlike structures knows as cupulae, which contain hairs connected to sensory cells called neuromasts. Cupulae and neuromasts are sensitive to the rate of water flow, providing the fish with information about its own movements as well as the swimming motions of other fish. Water displacement and turbulence are not sounds, however, and biologists disagree whether neuromasts are sensitive enough to be considered auditory systems.

Many fish species also make use of a labyrinth, or inner ear, similar to the inner ears of other vertebrates. In some species, such as the carps, the inner ear is in contact with a large hollow swim bladder that serves to amplify sounds, making the fish particularly sensitive to noise. Even those without such amplification can hear acutely. A fish's body is approximately the same density as the water it swims in, so sounds travel through the body unimpaired. The inner ear can therefore be located deep within the head and the sensory cells can be set in motion without the need for an outer canal to funnel sound. The otolith, or ear stone, rests atop sensory hairs connected to the sensory cells. When sound waves activate the otolith, which is denser than the rest of the fish, it moves out of phase with the inner ear. The difference bends the sensory hairs and stimulates the sensory cells.

Most animals with good hearing are good communicators as well. Hearing probably evolved as an adaptation to avoid predators and other dangers and became particularly acute among nocturnal animals. Songbirds, frogs, toads, and other animals that rely on well-developed vocal abilities to attract mates or defend territories developed ears that made it possible for them to hear those songs and calls. Among the birds, owls are unusual in having terrific hearing while making relatively few sounds themselves. The barn owl's ability to snatch small rodents even in total darkness is due in large part to the asymmetrical shape of its scooped oval face. The left ear is higher than the right, causing sound to arrive at one ear slightly sooner than the other and giving the owl the ability to pin-point the source of the sound with extraordinary accuracy.

Mammals, which generally have the best hearing in the animal kingdom, are unique in having pinnas, or external ear flaps. They are also the only vertebrates to have a middle ear composed of a chain of three small bones: the *malleus*, the *incus*, and the *stapes*. The malleus, sometimes known as the hammer, is fastened to the inside surface of the tympanic membrane. The incus, also called the anvil, is connected to the stapes (or stirrup), the smallest bone in the mammalian body. This complex arrangement of tiny bones transmits and amplifies sound from the eardrum to the cochlea of the inner ear.

Mammals living in deserts and other arid regions, such as the jack rabbit, often have large external ears because blood vessels near the surface of the ears are an effective way to rid their bodies of excess heat. Just as important, desert animals tend to be nocturnal, doing much of their foraging, grazing, and hunting at night, after the day has cooled. For them, acute hearing is a requirement of survival. The rabbit-eared bandicoot, an Australian marsupial, depends on its long, pointed ears to alert it to predators and to locate insects and small vertebrates while foraging at night; it folds the ears over its eyes, much as an insomniac tries to block out light. The kangaroo rats of the western United States, Canada, and Mexico have external ears no larger than most rodents, but they have highly developed inner ears that can amplify sounds as much as 100 times.

The most remarkable of all auditory systems belong to bats, dolphins, and a few other animals that use echolocation to navigate and detect prey. In echolocation, bursts of high frequency sounds are emitted. When those sounds bounce off an object and return to the sender, they create an audible "picture" of the object. Echolocation is so accurate that it allows dolphins and insect-eating bats (some fruit-eating bats can echolocate but their systems tend to be crude) to navigate more accurately with their hearing than many animals can with their eyes. A bat detects a moth at a distance of fifteen feet and determines in an instant the moth's size and the speed and direction of its flight, then adjust its own flight to intercept it. To maximize their echolocating abilities, many species of bats have developed very large ears and bizarre facial shapes that are effective at capturing sound waves.

Whether rudimentary, as in insects, or highly developed, as in primates, the sense of hearing fulfills several crucial functions. It warns of the approach of predators, detects prey, assists in locating potential mates, and in social animals helps maintain group cohesion. It may also assist birds and whales to navigate while they're migrating.

Hearing is an essential sense, critical to both predators and prey and finely honed among animals such as my son Aaron. When Aaron was fourteen years old he could hear the clink of silverware being set on the dining room table when he was upstairs in his bedroom with the door closed, studying chemistry, and listening to music on his headphones. It was a feat equivalent, by my reckoning, to a housecat in Cleveland detecting the pitter-patter of mouse feet in Brooklyn. Which makes it difficult to understand why Aaron had trouble hearing me when I asked for his help around the house.

"Aaron!"

"What!"

"I said take the garbage out!"

"Okay, jeez, you don't have to yell. I'm not deaf."

23
GET A WHIFF OF THIS

Winters are tough where I live, but we can usually count on a few days of mild weather in January. When water begins to drip from the eaves I wade through the snow to the nearest hill, climb to the top, and sniff. Sometimes, from far away, faint as a greeting shouted by a friend on a distant ridge, comes the first scent of spring. It's there for only a breath or two—an aroma of freshly turned earth, new blossoms, and rising sap— before winter closes in again. That brief scent conjures warm breezes, trickling meltwater, purple crocuses poking through yellow grass, the mossy, musky odor of earth exposed after months of snow cover. The promise it carries is sometimes all we need to get through the remaining weeks of hard weather.

Smell is the least appreciated, the least understood, and the least reliable of the human senses, yet it is the one most likely to arouse our passions. It dwells in the primitive, non-verbal center of our brain, inextricably linked to taste, in a swirling broth of feelings, associations, and memories—a place where language works only through metaphor and approximation. Compared to the olfactory abilities of many animals, we are pathetically incompetent. Some dogs have noses as much as a thousand times more sensitive than ours. Leaf-cutter ants are so attuned to the scent trails they lay down that a single milligram of trail pheromone is enough to lead a column of ants three times around the world. There are vast spectrums of odor we know nothing about.

No doubt there was a time when men and women gulped the air to check for predators and prey, to anticipate the weather, to gauge the chances for finding a suitable mate. Equipped with good eyes, good legs, and a good nose, a human had a reasonable chance of surviving. Smelling, like drawing pictures and playing the piano, seems to be one of those skills you use or lose.

One of the most sensitive human noses belonged to author and lecturer Helen Keller (1880-1968), who at age nineteen months contracted an illness now presumed to be either meningitis or scarlet fever that left her totally blind and deaf. In her memoir, *The Story of My Life*, Keller describes the importance of odors in her world:

> The sense of smell has told me of a coming storm hours before
> there was any sign of it visible. I notice first a throb of expectancy,
> a slight quiver, a concentration in my nostrils. As the storm draws
> near my nostrils dilate, the better to receive the flood of earth
> odors which seem to multiply and extend, until I feel the splash
> of rain on my cheek. As the tempest departs, receding farther and
> farther, the odors fade, become fainter and fainter, and die away
> beyond the bar of space...Masculine exhalations are, as a rule,
> stronger, more vivid, more widely differentiated than those of
> women. In the odor of young men there is something elemental, as
> of fire, storm, and salt sea. It pulsates with buoyancy and desire. It
> suggests all the things strong and beautiful and joyous and gives
> me a sense of physical happiness.

The olfactory sense is important even to those of us for whom it is only crudely developed. Without it food would taste only salty, sweet, bitter, or sour, and we would detect no distinguishable flavors. It's more important to us than we probably know. A thriving odor industry banks on the fact that we consciously or unconsciously prefer our bodies, homes, and consumer products to smell like flowers, pine needles, and animal musk. Malls and shopping centers inject perfumes into their heating and cooling systems to suffuse the air with odors that might make us more willing to part with our money. Employers have experimented with scents to increase worker productivity (lemon is said to perk up drowsy employees; rose keeps them from getting too frisky during lunch breaks). In Tokyo you can stop off at a health club after a stressful day at work and enjoy a thirty-minute aroma cocktail.

The idea that there is a connection between odors and health goes back to the Egyptians, who were among the first producers of perfume and who thought bad odors caused diseases. Fourteenth-century Europeans believed wearing a beak filled with aromatic spices could protect them from bubonic plague. Modern aromatherapists prescribe scents to cure everything from impotence to high blood pressure to cancer. Believers are convinced that the scent of eucalyptus fights bacteria, that lemon-grass oil cures acne, that rosemary slows memory loss, that saffron reduces the symptoms of a hangover. In France aromatherapy is so widely accepted that it is covered by health insurance. When your four-year-old comes down with a sore throat and cough, you can sooth her to sleep with a vaporizer puffing steam scented with oils of eucalyptus, peppermint, menthol, camphor, and lavender.

In evolutionary terms, the sense of smell is the oldest of the five senses, older than sight or hearing, older than taste and touch. It originated when aquatic organisms first began to swim in search of food and mates. Brains evolved on top of the limbic lobe, where the smell function is located. As a mammal inhales air, volatile molecules of odors in the air enter the respiratory system and adhere to mucus-covered membranes in the upper nasal passage. The precise process is not completely understood, but it appears that odor molecules, each with a distinctive shape, bind to odor receptors on the surface of the membranes. Like a key in a lock, each odor molecule lodges only in a similarly shaped receptor. The receptor then sends a signal to the brain, which identifies the fragrance as one of the 10,000 or so odors we're capable of differentiating.

The sense of smell serves other animals in ways we barely understand. Territorial mammals warn others of their species to stay away by depositing odors from scent glands located in the genital and anal regions, or on their feet, legs, or cheeks. Ants lay down chemical trails to and from food sources for other ants in their colony to follow. Mice and rats leave a trail of secretions along the ground so they can find their way back to their burrows. Impalas, springboks, and other herd mammals leap into the air when they see or scent a predator, kicking their feet and releasing alarm scents into the air from glands on their fetlocks.

A common odor is often established among animals living in the same colony, pack, or family. Female and young lions rub heads with others in their pride, greeting one another and probably merging smells to bond the group and aid with identification. Housecats rub against our legs, depositing scents from glands on their eyebrows and rumps, to make us more familiar and easily recognized. Individual mongooses rub their anal pouches on the same marking spot, spreading bacteria among family members to produce a shared odor. Social insects identify individuals with a kind of olfactory password. A honeybee that leaves its home hive carries a sample of the hive's individual fragrance in a scent sac. When the bee returns to the hive it lands at the hive entrance and opens the sac for inspection by guardian bees. If the sac contains unfamiliar odors the bee may be attacked; if the sac contains the specific blended scent of flowers, nectars, pollens, and resins unique to that hive the bee is allowed to enter.

Sex is probably the most powerful scent in the animal world. A male emperor moth extends its large, feathery antennae to detect the pheromones exuded by a female from as far as three miles away, and will fly unerringly upwind until he locates the source of that tantalizing perfume. Among mice, just a whiff from a nearby male will trigger reproductive hormones in a female and cause her uterus to begin swelling. Within twenty minutes she comes into heat. If she is already pregnant when she comes in contact with a male, the embryos are aborted or absorbed into her body and she conceives again.

A critical scent bond is established between many mothers and their young almost immediately after birth. Human mothers can detect the odor of their own babies within a few days of birth. Many mammals will reject young other than their own, but farmers long ago discovered that ewes whose young have died can be convinced to raise orphaned lambs if the orphans wear the skins of the dead lambs.

Odors figure into a variety of defense systems. The active ingredient in a skunk's spray is so potent it can be detected by humans in amounts that are virtually immeasurable: about .000,000,000,000,07 of an ounce. The cloud of inky fluid secreted by an octopus, squid, or cuttlefish contains a compound that dulls the olfactory organs of predators. In the western United States there is an old cowboy tradition of encircling a bedroll at night with a lariat to create a fence against rattlesnakes. A herpetologist I spoke with admitted that rattlers are repelled by human odor, and that they might hesitate to cross a rope that's been handled by a man or woman, but he wouldn't care to test the theory.

Extraordinary feats of scenting are everywhere. A salmon remembers the unique chemical composition of the river where it was born and can detect a few parts per million of its scent. After two or three years at sea it traces the scent through hundreds of miles of ocean and returns unerringly to its home river to spawn. Polar bears have been observed detecting and following the scent of a dead seal twenty miles away. Black bears and grizzlies that have been immobilized with drugs and transported to remote areas can detect familiar scents and return hundreds of miles over unfamiliar territory to their home ranges.

The bloodhound that the police use to track a lost child or an escaped convict has up to 150 square centimeters of smell-receptive membrane in its nose (compared to about four square centimeters in humans). It keys in on a variety of olfactory clues, including the odor of the approximately fifty million skin cells a human sheds each day and the unmistakable aura of human sweat that is left in the air wherever we go and even filters down through the soles of our shoes.

The U.S. Department of Agriculture maintains a "Beagle Brigade" consisting of highly trained dogs that work with human handlers to inspect airline luggage for prohibited fruit, plants, meat, and the pests and diseases they carry. Beagles make great inspectors because of their gentle nature and willingness to work for treats, but especially because they have great noses. Every beagle is equipped with an estimated 220 million scent receptors (humans have about five million), and has a remarkable capacity for remembering every odor it smells. Some Beagle Brigade dogs have memorized the scents of as many as fifty different meats and agricultural products.

Every autumn I tramp through aspen thickets with friends and their hunting dogs and am always astonished by how skilled the dogs are at finding birds. To my nose the scent of a woodcock and grouse is so faint that I can detect it only when I hold the bird close to my nose. It's an odor vaguely reminiscent of mushrooms, or like cheese and loamy earth. Yet the dogs can locate the birds where they hide, camouflaged and unmoving, in thick underbrush in an aromatic forest, from distances of sometimes hundreds of feet. The setters and retrievers race through the woods, nostrils snuffling, and when they catch the scent of a bird behave in specific manners regarded by hunters as "birdy"—locking into a nose-to-the-ground point or sniffing the ground furiously in ever-tightening circles. I'm a barely competent hunter, so the birds usually escape, but not because the dogs are unable to find them.

Even the human nose, poor as it is, can perform amazing gymnastics. A hint of lilac perfume in a crowded store takes me back to high school in the 1970s, when certain girls favored that most purple of perfumes. I'm sensitive to the smells of apples and burning leaves, am romanced by the scent of books new and old. On a good day I can smell rain before it arrives and can catch a whiff of the sweet fern growing along the Boardman River when I'm still a mile away. Some days, when the wind is from the right direction and my nose is in top form, I can stand on a snow-drifted hill and catch April in January.

RETINA

FOVEA

OPTIC

NERVES

LENS

24
TO SEE FOR MILES

Autumn is the best season for seeing. Wind and rain have scrubbed the air so clean that the afternoon light seems somehow burnished and at night the stars burn with a sharp and steady brilliance. Winter is approaching fast and with it will come a certain amount of sensory impoverishment. We don't want to waste a second of that autumn light.

One fall afternoon my friend Norris McDowell and I were driving slowly along back roads in the Upper Peninsula of Michigan when he said, "I love October. It's so damned arrogant." I couldn't have agreed more. The maples and aspens were brilliant that day—a shameless burst of reds and yellows—and the hills were pure swagger. Norris braked the truck and pointed at something across a broad meadow. I raised my binoculars and saw it too: a whitetail buck with a magnificent rack of antlers. The deer stood in a shaft of sunlight, one of those golden rays people once thought could be climbed like a ladder to heaven. The sight was unforgettable: a majestic whitetail against a backdrop of autumn colors, the best of the season brought vividly to the eye. I only wish I could have seen it without magnification.

At the risk of sounding like a guy obsessed with his past glories, I have to admit that in my youth I had pretty good eyes. No, I'm being too modest: I had great eyes. Back then I would have been the first to see that buck standing across the field, and would have been able to count the eight points on his antlers, just as I was always the first to read a distant traffic sign or to spot a hawk circling high on a thermal current. Now, I don't see well in the dark and need to wear reading glasses to keep the letters from backstroking off the page.

Eyes—those windows to the soul—are much more than just the mind's portholes. We see what our eyes are designed to see: a narrow band of light waves reflecting off objects. Usually, when you compare sensory skills in the animal kingdom, humans fall short. But we've got relatively acute eyesight, a legacy from our tree-dwelling ancestors who probably did not need outstanding noses to locate fruit hanging from nearby branches and could not hear much up there with the wind rustling the leaves. Eyes became our most valuable sense for survival, just as they are for most birds. Vision is so important to birds that their eyes are much larger in proportion to the size of their skulls than those of most animals.

Like all predators, humans have forward-facing eyes that allow each eye's field of vision to overlap, giving us excellent depth perception. This so-called binocular vision is valuable for focusing on distant objects, but it leaves us blindsided. Prey animals, in contrast, usually have eyes that are set back on their skulls, allowing them, in some cases, to have 360-degree vision. Birds such as pigeons and doves have great peripheral sight to protect against predators, but because they have little or no binocular vision they are unable to tell how far away the danger lurks. To compensate, they must move their heads back and forth and up and down to judge distance based on the way perspective changes against a background.

Eyes can be very simple or very complicated. Among the simplest are the light-sensitive cells in the skin of earthworms. Visible only under a microscope, these cells merely detect the difference between light and dark, which serves the light-shunning worms well enough. A slightly more complex organ is the eyespot of the planarian, or flatworm. Each spot consists of a cluster of half a dozen light-sensitive cells in a cuplike recession lined with black pigment. The pigment prevents light from reaching the cells from any direction except the front, allowing the planarian to sense where the light comes from. More sophisticated yet is the eye of the chambered nautilus, a marine mollusk whose anatomy has changed little in 400 million years. Its deeply recessed eye pit has an opening that can be widened or narrowed to adjust the amount of light that enters. It works much like a simple pinhole camera, letting in light rays and projecting them onto light-receptive cells at the back of the pit.

But pinhole cameras have serious limitations. They are effective only in very bright lights. Widen the opening to allow in more light and too much enters, causing the image to blur. Narrow the opening to sharpen focus and the image dims. Photographers solved this problem by using a lens, an idea borrowed from the eye design of vertebrates and many worms and snails. The "lens eye" has a relatively large aperture with a flexible lens fixed inside it. The lens refracts, or bends, light rays gathered from outside and focuses them on the retina, the light-sensitive layer of cells at the back of the eye, where the optic nerve is located. The image arrives at the retina upside down, but is immediately righted when the message reaches the brain.

If we could see through the eyes of other animals, we would behold a world dressed in spectacular variations of color and detail. Equipped with the six or eight eyes of a spider, we would see vague peripheral shapes and a focused, short-sighted view straight ahead. The head and front legs of an aphid, say, would be magnified to the size of an elephant, while its rear legs would recede in blurry distance. If we borrowed the compound eyes of a housefly, we would see little in the distance, but everything in a close circle around us would be in equal focus. If we saw through the eyes of a cormorant, two worlds would be equally clear: an aquatic world made brilliant with the flashing silver glints of baitfish, and a surface world of air and light. If we saw what a honeybee sees, blossoms that human eyes perceive as plain white or pale yellow would be a violet color so bright they would glow like neon and would be traced with dark lines, like directional arrows pointing to the bounty of nectar at the center.

Many vertebrates, humans included, have an area on the retina where light receptors and nerve connections are heavily concentrated. This area of ultra-sensitive sight, called the fovea, varies in size and shape from animal to animal. In humans it is circular and centered, allowing us to discern the details within complex, cluttered scenes. Gazelles on the African savanna have a narrow, elongated fovea that provides extra sensitivity for scanning the horizon in search of predators. Birds of prey have two fovea per eye, creating a sort of zoom lens which allows them to see their prey from great distances and swoop down upon them with pin-point accuracy.

Familiarity tends to blind us to most of the sublime visions of our ordinary days. Ralph Waldo Emerson suggested that if the stars were visible only once in a thousand years, they would be the most extraordinary event of every millennium. When the essayist Edward Hoagland underwent surgery to restore his sight after several years of being legally blind, he reawakened to "the miracle of the streaming clouds, the blowing grass, the leaping birds, the upspread trees… I wouldn't believe how golden the sunshine was, how softly green each leaf, or how radiant the city night could be."

If one purpose in life, as Henry James said, is to be a person on whom nothing is lost, the primary tool for the job is the eye. In zoos, sporting arenas, and movie theaters we binge on images, drinking them in greedily. We want those images branded on our retinas forever. We want to remember the brassy light of an autumn day, the way it glances off the surface of a lake and lights the hills with color. We want whitecaps on the ocean and the reckless plummet of a pelican. We want spiderwebs glistening with dewdrops and storm clouds towering above the Plains.

At a party once, a few of my friends challenged one another to choose the animals we would like to be. It surprised no one that playful Mike would be a river otter, or that graceful Marcy would choose to be a cat, or that prankster Craig would be a coyote. Nobody shared my wish to be a raptor. I wanted to be a northern harrier or a peregrine or a bald eagle—not, as I was accused, so I could hunt rodents or be held up as an emblem of national pride, but because I want keen eyesight and soaring wings, want to climb the sky and see for miles.

25
AGING GRACEFULLY

Nick was a very wise five-year-old. He told me once that time was indeed relative, and that in the final tally the hours we spend having fun don't count against us. That's why time passed so quickly, he explained, when he played with his buddy, Jeff, and why the day is broken up into "long hours" and "little hours." Since many of my own hours seem to be long ones, I took what he said seriously. And sure enough, the hours I spend having fun with the people I love, doing the things that light us up, pass in a twinkling. It makes me think of the plucky ninety-nine-year-old narrator of Allan Gurganus's novel, *Oldest Living Confederate Widow Tells All*, who says, "He who laughs, lasts."

Biologists call the aging process *senescence* and define it as "age-associated decline in the individual's physical capacities." That decline causes a corresponding increase in the chances an animal will fall victim to accidents, illness, and predators. Older individuals are more likely to die simply because they are not as agile and alert as younger animals, and because their immune systems are not as effective in fighting disease and infection. Among humans, the probability of dying doubles approximately every eight years of life. For baboons it doubles every three years; for

Virginia opossums, every eight months. Unlike mammals, wild birds tend to die at approximately the same rate regardless of age, perhaps because, some researchers theorize, the demands of flight are so unforgiving (a weak flyer is a dead flyer).

Though biologists know what aging is, and know with certainty that it leads to death, no one can say how it happens. We seem to age from our cells outward, and some research suggests that on a strictly cellular level it might be possible to delay aging indefinitely. Ponce de León's search for a fountain of youth seems downright modest compared to the efforts of laboratory researchers seeking an "aging gene" they hope can be clipped from a string of DNA to give us perpetual youth.

There are two basic theories that attempt to explain why we age. The older is the "rate-of-living" theory, which was formalized in 1907 by German biologist Max Rubner. Rubner theorized that animals of every kind begin life with a finite amount of vital energy and that their life spans vary according to how quickly they burn that energy. Thus large animals with slow metabolisms live long lives, while small animals with rapid metabolisms die sooner. The popular interpretation was we begin life with a stockpile of approximately the same number of heartbeats.

On the surface the evidence in support of rate-of-living seemed indisputable: Elephants are big and slow and live many years; tiny shrews burn with a metabolic rate that is red-hot by comparison and survive only a year or two. Yet there are gaps in the scenario that have caused most biologists to dismiss it in favor of theories based on genetics and evolution. One of the classic arguments against rate-of-living is that it does not address the fact that birds, with metabolic rates much faster than most mammals of similar size, typically live twice as long as those mammals, despite using vastly more energy. Even in the safety of a laboratory, a mouse can't live much beyond three years. Song sparrows of about the same size have been found to live as long as eleven years in the wild.

A bird may reach ripe old age because the ability to fly gives it an immediate advantage over predators. Flight is an effective defense and seems to have created a genetic predisposition toward longer lives. The flying squirrel of the eastern U.S., though a glider rather than a true flier, has lived up to seventeen years in captivity; the similarly sized chipmunk lives only about eight years. Bats have the ability—astonishing in mammals so small—to live to the age of thirty years or more. Rate-of-living advocates once argued that bats live so long because they hibernate during cold weather and lower their body temperatures while sleeping during the day, thereby conserving their stock of vital energy. That argument does not explain, however, why tropical fruit bats, which do not hibernate, also live much longer than similar-sized flightless mammals.

Other defenses, such as the turtle's shell and the porcupine's quills, may likewise be responsible for making those animals unusually long-lived. Now and then someone discovers an ancient moss-backed turtle with an inscription carved on its shell. Turtle shells are the subway-station walls of the animal world, blank canvases irresistible to expressive people with pocket knives. The carved message might read, "Dan Boone was here, July 1764," or "Reg loves Linda 6/14/48," creating a small sensation in the local newspaper and a bigger one on Facebook, but the dates are often suspect, and some skepticism is understandable. Nonetheless, desert tortoises, snapping turtles, and box turtles have all lived fifty or more years in captivity. The longevity record for reptiles, in fact, probably goes to one of three turtles. The first was a giant tortoise said to have been captured as an adult and to have lived in a British fort on the island of Mauritius, in the Indian Ocean, more than 150 years before dying when it fell through a gun emplacement. Another was a radiated tortoise, purported to have been presented to the king of Tonga by Captain James Cook around 1775, and which died in 1965. The third was a giant land tortoise, named Harriet, that DNA testing proved was born about 1830, was captured in the Galapagos Islands in 1835 by none other than Charles Darwin, and finally died in 2006 at the age of 176 as the most famous and beloved resident of the Australia Zoo in Queensland.

A turtle's formidable defenses not only protect the individual as it faces the hazards of daily living, but may create, in the words of Harvard biology professor Steven Austad, an "evolutionary history of increased safety" that passes beneficial genes from generation to generation. That history results, after many generations, in individual turtles whose cells are programmed to remain youthful.

Studies of animal longevity have been frequently marred by exaggeration. For centuries a German museum exhibited the skeleton of a northern pike said to have been caught in 1497. The fish bore an identification ring dating back to Emperor Frederick II, suggesting it was about 250 years old when it died. Ultimately, the fish was found to be a fraud, its skeleton composed of the bones of several pike.

But reliable sources point to many extraordinary old-timers. Among birds it's generally true that larger species live the longest. Bald eagles, Canada geese, and trumpeter swans have all been known to live from twenty-two to twenty-four years in the wild. Brown pelicans can live nineteen years, and the much smaller blue jay has reached sixteen years. The record for a bird in the wild is probably a Laysan albatross that lived more than thirty-seven years.

Birds in captivity are regularly fed and are usually safe from predators, so it's not surprising that they tend to live longer than wild birds. A Canada goose has lived thirty-three years in captivity. Northern cardinals have lived to twenty-two years, and canaries to more than twenty years. The oldest known bird in captivity was a sulfur-crested cockatoo that lived well into its eighties.

Other animals are not always easy to age, but some are documented. An American alligator in the Dresden Zoological Garden lived to be approximately fifty-six years old. A common European toad was said to live as a pet for thirty-six years, but the documentation is suspicious. Better records list an American bullfrog that survived in captivity for sixteen years, a hellbender that lived for twenty-nine years, and a giant Japanese salamander that resided in a zoological park in Leyden, Netherlands until its death at age fifty-five.

The annual growth bands on clam shells reveal that some clams can live hundreds of years. In fact, the world's oldest known animal was an ocean quahog, the same type of clam that often ends up in a bowl of chowder. This particular quahog was collected while still alive in 2006, along with about 200 other randomly dredged clams, from the bottom of the Atlantic Ocean near the coast of Iceland. It was promptly frozen, killing it, and transported to a laboratory for analysis. Researchers at the lab counted the bands on the clam's shell and were stunned to discover that it had lived 507 years. That means it was born in 1499, while Leonardo da Vinci was working on the "Mona Lisa," and a few months after Christopher Columbus returned from his third voyage to the New World. The quahog, nicknamed "Ming" because it was born while the Ming dynasty still ruled China, was collected at random and was no larger in size than other clams around it. Almost certainly there exist other clams in the oceans that are even older.

At more than 150 years, sturgeon are probably the longest-lived freshwater fish. The longest-lived marine fish is likely to be the rougheye rockfish of the northeast Pacific. Biologists analyzing the annual growth rings in the rougheye's otalith, or ear bone, have found individuals of this depth-loving species to be as old as 205 years. Biogerontologists are curious to know why other members of the same genus live only about twelve years. What sets the rougheye apart? Is there a genetic clue here that might help explain why humans and other animals age?

The idea that aging is genetically programmed naturally suggests that some sort of clock is ticking away. Evidence of such a timer was found in the late 1970s by researcher Leonard Hayflick at Children's Hospital Medical Center in Oakland, California. In experiments with human cells kept alive in tissue cultures, Hayflick discovered that cell nuclei from middle-aged humans will divide about twenty times before they die, while cells from human embryos divide about fifty times. He concluded that the older the person, the less often his or her cells divide, and thus it is the nucleus of a cell that "ages."

As usual, scientific explanations offer little comfort against reality. You probably don't have to be reminded that among humans the signs of aging include gray hair, wrinkled skin, loss of muscle tone, stooped posture, brittle bones, weakening of eyes, and a tendency to retell old stories even after everyone is sick of hearing them. My wife and children started telling me when I was barely in my thirties and still bursting with youthful vigor that I exhibited many of those symptoms and was developing an especially severe case of the latter one. So be it. Much of the secret to aging gracefully is learning to accept the consequences with dignity. Besides, those stories are pretty good, and definitely worth retelling.

As impatient as we can be with the physical symptoms of aging, it's therapeutic to remember that old age is uncommon in nature. Every creature gets older, but few animals other than humans and house pets age much beyond the first signs of senescence. Most die off as soon as they start losing strength and speed.

Maybe I'm imagining it, but some days I can feel my nuclei growing older by the minute. My hair grays at a detectable rate, gravity tugs at my waist, and I keep finding strange hairs sprouting from my ears. Like everyone, I try to find comfort where I can. It helps to cultivate a cheerful attitude, to spend a lot of time outdoors, to hang out with young humans and old dogs. Old dogs are especially therapeutic. I love their serene disregard of all things temporary and frivolous, the way their loyalties grow solid and rich and unconditional, the way they can doze for hours in the sun, their legs kicking as if dreaming of puppyhood and rabbit chases. Wake an old dog gently, lure him with a hand tapped invitingly on your knee, and he pries himself up, groaning and stiff. He always comes to you, tail wagging, ready for one more game. Throw a ball (but not too far) and be patient while he takes his time finding it and returning with it. Time is a greedy and heartless bastard and there's not a thing we can do about it, but those minutes of search and retrieve don't count against him—or you.

PART IV

ANIMAL MYTHS AND LEGENDS

26
CALL OF THE MERMAID

I've you've ever seen a manatee floating in a Florida canal you know what a stretch of the imagination it must be to think it looks anything like a mermaid. That pale, loaflike, almost hairless mammal more closely resembles a giant insect larva than the sexy half-human sirens of folklore and popular culture.

But early mariners remained at sea for months at a time, usually in the company only of men, so no doubt they saw something womanlike out there. Biologists long ago considered manatees and their relatives plausible enough sources for the mermaid legend to name their order Sirenia, for the ancient Greek Sirens who were the mermaid's mythological forerunners. The subject gets strange—gets absolutely psychological—when you consider that Sirens and mermaids were accused of luring sailors to their deaths, something a gentle manatee could never do.

Legends of mermaids and mermen (folklorists group them as merfolk) go way back and often are linked with a belief widespread in the Middle Ages that every creature on land has an equivalent in the sea. There were horses and sea horses, dogs and dogfish, lions and sea lions. Why not men and mermen or women and mermaids?

An early prototype of the mermaid was a Babylonian fertility goddess named Atargatis, who dates back to about 5,000 B.C. and was personified as both good and destructive, a contradictory nature that would later be standard in most merfolk legends. In the second century A.D. the Greek writer Lucian described a drawing of the original fertility goddess Atargatis as distinctly mermaid-like: "...for in the upper half she is a woman, but from the waist to the lower extremities runs in the tail of a fish." From a Babylonian goddess she evolved into Aphrodite, Greek goddess of love, and Venus, the Roman goddess of love. In those forms she was without a fishlike tail, which was given instead to the Tritons, Aphrodite's male escorts in the sea, and to their female companions, the Tritonids.

The Sirens of Greek mythology contributed much to mermaid legends. Those carnivorous sea nymphs had the heads of women and the bodies of birds and inhabited certain Mediterranean islands where they would go to the shore and sing such alluring music that sailors could not resist them. Once the mariners ventured near, however, their ships were wrecked on rocks and the men devoured. Jason and the Argonauts avoided that disaster by listening instead to the lyre music of Orpheus, which was loud enough to drown out the Sirens. In the Odyssey, Odysseus saved his ship and crew from the Sirens by ordering his men to lash him to the mast and to plug their own ears with wax.

By the Middle Ages, European folklore had brought mermaids down to Earth, making them mortal like elves and fairies and giving them a variety of magical powers. In many folktales, it was bad luck to accept a gift from a mermaid, and if she was offended (by, say, a human who refused to accept a gift), she would cause floods and other natural disasters. For a mariner to merely glimpse a mermaid was an omen of shipwreck, but you could never be sure you had actually seen one. Sometimes mermaids would assume human form and prowl through towns and seaports. Sometimes men married them, but it took a crafty groom to pull it off. First he had to steal something the mermaid valued—her cap, her comb, or her mirror— and hide it in a secure place. As long as the object remained hidden the mermaid was forced to remain his wife. But if she ever recovered her possession she would escape immediately back into the sea.

Other versions of the legend include a German mermaid named Lorelei who stationed herself on a cliff 433 feet above a narrow, twisting section of the Rhine River and sang in a voice so lovely it distracted boaters and caused them to crash into the rocks. Gerald Lyon in his 1481 bestiary, *Creatures Moralisees*, described a mermaid enticing mariners to their deaths with frankly sexual appeal. As a ship passed, she would frolic nude in the sea beside it and call up to the sailors to join her in the water. If a lust-maddened man dived in, the maiden would transform into a monster and devour him. In a French variation of a legend found throughout Europe during the Middle Ages, the angelic Melusina appeared before Count Raymound in human form but changed back to her actual half-human, half-fish form on Saturdays. He fell in love with her and asked her to marry, and she agreed, but only on the condition that he never look at her during the one day of the week when she resumed her mermaid form. Inevitably there came a Saturday when he could not resist spying on her, whereupon she returned to the sea and spent the rest of eternity tormenting sailors in a shrieking voice that foretold wrecks.

In the Caribbean, where belief in supernatural water creatures remains common, mermaids have long been considered male creatures of the sea, while faerymaids are female inhabitants of freshwater rivers and springs. Both make their homes in caverns under the water. They are tricksters possessing magical powers and can be dangerous to humans, stealing their shadows, driving them mad, or luring them to their underwater dwellings. If a human eats any food offered to them while visiting one of those dwellings, he or she is condemned to remain below water forever.

Elsewhere in the New World legends of mermaids were less likely to emphasize the creatures' supernatural attributes. More often they were regarded as actual fauna, not much different from the newly discovered and equally wondrous bison, grizzly bear, and other animals found on the vast new continent.

Most of us know, of course, that mermaids don't exist and never did. Unlike the Loch Ness Monster, Sasquatch, and visitors from other planets, merfolk seldom inspire true believers to come forward and argue for their existence. Yet in the past there have been many eyewitnesses who were convinced that the creatures were real.

Perhaps the most famous was Christopher Columbus. During his first voyage to the New World, while sailing east from the settlement he established on the island of Hispaniola, he reported matter-of-factly in his log that he and his crew had sighted "three sirens that rose high out of the sea, but were not as beautiful as they are represented." Many commentators have assumed he saw manatees; others have theorized that Columbus saw a trio of the now extinct Caribbean monk seal rising in the water to watch the *Nina* as she passed.

Another West Indies mermaid was reported by Captain John Smith in the seventeenth century. Smith admitted being smitten with the animal and noted it had "large eyes, rather too round, a finely-shaped nose, a little too short, well-formed ears, rather too long, and her long green hair imparted to her an original character." But when the mermaid swam near Smith, he was startled to see that she "gave way to fish" below the waist.

A Captain Whitbourne, sailing to North America in 1610, claimed he saw a mermaid as he approached St. John's, Newfoundland. By his account, the creature swam toward his ship "looking cheerfully as it had been a woman, by the Face, Eyes, Nose, Mouth, Ears, Neck and Forehead." When it tried to scramble aboard a nearby vessel crewmen promptly clobbered it on the head with an oar. Whitbourne concluded by writing, "Whether it were a mermaid or no...I leave it for others to judge."

While sailing up the Hudson River in 1609, Henry Hudson filed this report in his journal: "This evening one of our company, looking overboard, saw a mermaid, and, calling up some of the company to see her, one more of the crew came up, and by that time she was close to the ship's side, looking earnestly on the men. A little after that a sea came and overturned her. From the navel upward, her back and breasts were like a woman's, as they saw her; her body was as big as one of us, her skin very white, and long hair hanging down her back, of color black. In her going down they saw her tail, which was like the tail of a porpoise, speckled like a mackerel."

A merchant and fur trader named Venant St. German claimed that in May 1782 he saw a mermaid in Lake Superior. Under oath in Montreal he later reported in a deposition: "...[A] little before sunset, the evening being clear and serene...the deponent happened to turn towards the lake, when he observed, about an acre or three quarters of an acre distant from the bank where he stood, an animal in the water, which appeared to him to have the upper part of its body, above the waist, formed exactly like that of a human being. It had the half of its body out of the water, and the novelty of so extraordinary a spectacle excited his attention, and led him to examine it carefully. The body of the animal seemed to him about the size of that of a child of seven or eight years of age, with one of its arms extended and elevated in the air. The hand appeared to be composed of fingers exactly similar to those of a man...the features of the countenance... bore an exact resemblance to those of the human face."

In his 1827 book, *A Voyage Toward the South Pole Performed in the Years 1822-24, Containing an Examination of the Antarctic Sea*, the English seal hunter James Weddell included an account of a mermaid observed by a member of his crew. While sleeping on the shore of one of the South Shetland Island, the man was awakened by "...a noise resembling human cries...He walked the beach a few steps. On searching around, he saw an object lying on a rock, a dozen yards from the shore, at which he was somewhat frightened. The face and shoulders appeared of human form, and of a reddish colour; over the shoulders hung long green hair; the tail resembled that of a seal, but the extremities of the arms he could not see distinctly. The creature continued to make a musical noise while he gazed about two minutes, and on perceiving him it disappeared in an instant." It seems odd that Weddell would include the story in his book if he had even a slight suspicion that the sailor had seen a seal (with, perhaps, aquatic weeds or algae draped over its head), especially since Weddell was an experienced sealer and a careful observer of wildlife—he is credited as the discoverer of the seal that still bears his name—and he was traveling in a region where seals were abundant.

Attempts at rational explanations for mermaid almost always center around manatees, dugongs, seals, and walruses. That makes sense, claim debunkers, since those aquatic mammals are vaguely human in appearance and are found in many of the waters where merfolk sightings have been most common. But reports of dugong and manatees nursing their calves in distinctly human fashion, floating on their backs with the young cradled on their bellies, are simply wrong. Sirenians nurse their young underwater, with the calves suspended beneath them.

In Ireland and Scotland, where belief in mermaids and fairies has diminished in recent decades, many of their supernatural powers have been transferred to seals. Seals, according to the folklore of the British Isles, are capable of talking, prophesying, weeping, singing, and giving aid to wrecked or stranded mariners, and can periodically remove their skins and go ashore to walk about in human form. It's thought that a seal remains in human form as long as it is out of skin, but if someone discovers the skin the seal must do whatever it is bid to do, including marrying a human and bearing children.

Like a lot of legendary creatures, mermaids are complex. The folklorist Horace Beck, author of *Folklore of the Sea*, says their complexity is a result of being a "fractured mythology" glued together from many sources of folklore, mythology, and legend. Perhaps, too, mermaids legends are a reflection of the oceans themselves: beautiful, mysterious, and lethal. Maybe it is our feelings about the oceans that are complicated. The call of the sea might be very different from the call of a Siren, but both are difficult to ignore and both can have dire consequences.

The world is big and it hides wonders. The seas, especially, are crammed with oddities even stranger than a naked humanlike animal with a finned tail. The netting of a coelacanth by a South African fishing trawler in 1938, 65 million years after its supposed extinction, is often cited as evidence of how much is yet to be learned about life in the oceans. If the coelacanth can be found alive, the reasoning goes, why not other presumably extinct animals? Who's to say that many of the legendary creatures of the sea are not based on sightings of rare but real animals?

The potential for such wonders excites us. We love stories that raise the hairs on our necks and are willing to believe even the most outlandish of them. In Japan in the nineteenth century artisans manufactured thousands of conterfeit mermaids from stuffed monkey skins sewn to fish tails and sold them to gullible sailors. P.T. Barnum, of "there's a sucker born every minute" fame, used a similar ruse during the 1870s to separate thousands of credulous yokels from their paychecks. They rushed to stand in line to see the shriveled and naked corpse of a mermaid that Barnum shrewdly kept hidden in a private viewing room. An Englishman named Robert Hawker pulled off a spectacular hoax in 1825 by stripping naked, wrapping the lower half of his body in an oilskin tail, and swimming to a prominent rock off the shore of Cornwall. He spent several nights on the rock, combing seaweed from his hair, looking into a mirror, and singing. The performance was convincing enough to attract enormous crowds. Hawker ended the hoax by singing a mighty rendition of "God Save the King" and diving from the rock and out of sight.

Whenever a legend or myth persists you can be sure there is some universal need for it. Where there is mythological smoke, after all, there is often psychological fire. Perhaps, in the case of mermaids and sea monsters, the fire is fueled by our powerful and contradictory feelings about the oceans themselves. The sea can inspire us and it can terrify us. It is both unimaginably rich with life and dreadfully indifferent to death. It gives us sustenance with one turn of the tide and takes our lives with the next. Stand on its shore at night and it seems as vast and terrifying as the universe itself. We love it and it scares the hell out of us.

Such a powerful mix of emotions demands symbols we can grab onto. Besides, we like a good story. This one has all the elements of a blockbuster: half-naked women, men in mortal struggle with their animal urges, the sea providing a background of mood and music, its rhythms as pervasive and assuring as the beating of our own hearts.

Oryx gazella

PERSIAN ORIENTAL EVROPEAN

NARWHAL

27
THE FABULOUS
UNICORN

We didn't set out to do it, but the responsibilities of parenthood made my wife and me into shameless deceivers of our children. For several Christmases running, Nick asked if there was really a Santa Claus, but we managed to duck the question. Finally he backed us into a corner and asked again, and we replied, rather lamely, "Yes. If you believe in him." Nick immediately asked if there were monsters living under his bed. When we assured him there were not, he said, "But I believe in them." It's hard to argue against such firm logic. "That's different," Gail said. "It applies only to happy things."

A lie, of course, but one for which we can be forgiven, I think. It reminds me of the lines by Emily Dickinson: "The Possible's slow fuse is lit/By the Imagination." All we have to do is imagine bedroom monsters and Santa Claus, and the slow fuse of possibility is set sputtering.

The same goes for the animals of myth and legend. I've been reading a lot about unicorns lately, and they seem to be particularly ripe for possibility. I asked Nick what he thought of them, and he replied, "Sort of like horses with horns." He was so matter-of-fact about it that I wondered if he'd been seeing them all along, maybe beneath a full moon, prancing in daisy rings in the backyard.

For centuries unicorns were among the easiest of fabulous animals to believe in, probably because they seemed so likely to be real. Stripped of magic, a unicorn is no more bizarre than a giraffe or an elephant. It should exist. Why not a graceful, single-horned mammal related to horses, deer, and antelopes? It's easy to imagine it being a shy and rarely seen forest dweller like the okapi, or able to leap amazing distances like a pronghorn. It could disappear from sight, but only as mysteriously as a white-tailed deer that fades silently into a cedar grove. It would be no more fabulous than the klipspringer of Africa, a toylike antelope that springs from rock to rock and lands on all four hooves on a spot the size of a silver dollar.

Unicorn legends date back thousands of years. In ancient China, a creature with scales on its body and a single horn growing from its forehead was said to appear before the emperor Fu Xi as he meditated about the fleeting nature of existence. Markings on the creature's back inspired the emperor to invent written language and to put a temporary stay on the transitoriness of life. From then on, the unicorn was considered by the Chinese to be a symbol of gentleness and longevity.

The legend spread west, first appearing in print in the fourth century B.C. in the writings of the Greek physician Ctesias. By then unicorns were usually described as so large, powerful, and ferocious that even rhinos and elephants ran from them in terror.

Ctesias spent seventeen years tending to the medical needs of Darius II of Persia, in the meantime collecting travelers' tales from foreign lands. In his book based upon those tales he described the unicorn as follows:

> There are in India certain wild asses which are as large as horses and even darker. Their bodies are white, their heads dark red, and their eyes dark blue. They have a horn in the middle of the forehead that is about a foot and a half in length... Those who drink from these horns, made into drinking vessels, are not

subject, they say, to convulsions or to the falling sickness. Indeed, they are immune even to poisons...The animal is exceedingly swift and powerful, so that no creature, neither the horse nor any other, can overtake it.

Ctesias's description of this mysterious creature was so frequently repeated that many people became convinced that it must exist. During the third century B.C., seventy-two Jewish scholars in Alexandria set out to translate the Bible from Hebrew into Greek and found in the Hebrew version several references to an animal called the "re'em." None of the scholars knew what a re'em was, though they understood from its description that it was a large, horned beast of fierce demeanor. Modern scholars believe the re'em to be a species of now-extinct buffalo, but the Alexanderian scholars chose to rename the creature monoceros, which was later Latinized as unicornis.

Once it was sanctioned by the Bible, the unicorn took on more significance than it had in ancient Greece. It was particularly important in the popular bestiaries of the Middle Ages, where unicorns were held up as paragons of moral rectitude and were sometimes equated with Christ.

In their book *Dragons and Unicorns, A Natural History*, Paul and Karin Johnsgard give unicorns the zoological attention they deserve. This delightful exercise in whimsy traces the ancestry of unicorns to early antelopes of the Pleistocene (not horses, as is usually assumed), and points out that they are closely related to the even-toed ungulates and should be grouped with modern antelopes because their horns grow continuously, are not shed, and are found on both males and females.

According to the Johnsgards, there have been three species of single-horned Monoceros during historical times. The largest was the karkadann, or Persion unicorn, *M. tyrannus*. Now considered extinct, it was native to the grasslands and deserts of Persia, India, and perhaps northeastern Africa. It was a fierce beast, able to kill elephants and rhinos by driving its horn into their bellie, and probably resembled the oryxes, large antelopes of Asia and northern Africa that have often been mistaken for unicorns.

Indeed, when they stand in profile, their two horns appear to be a single horn. The karkadann could bellow so loudly that birds and other animals fled in terror at the sound.

The second species in the Johnsgards' fanciful natural history is the Asian unicorn, *M. orientalis*, or ki-lin (kirin in Japan), which is native to most of eastern Asia, including Japan, Korea, China, and parts of Tibet. It is the size of a small stag, with a shaggy tail, brightly spotted coat in patterns of red, yellow, blue, white, and black, and a blunt horn. Its call is sweet and melodious, and sometimes likened to a silver bell. Because the animal is extremely shy, it is the least often seen of the unicorns and little is known of its habits.

M. europus, the European unicorn, is the most familiar around the world because it is the species most often illustrated in tapestries, books, and posters. It stands about three and a half feet at the shoulder and weighs up to 100 pounds. The horn is long, slender, and tightly twisted, with a sharp point. Its call is described as a "sad wail."

Ancient authorities usually agreed that unicorns were too shrewd, quick, and dangerous to be easily captured. But on occasion they could be caught, most reliably by using a virgin human female as bait. It was thought that the unicorn was so enraptured by a pure-hearted maiden that it would approach her without fear, lay its head in her lap, and fall instantly into sleep. The young woman and others were then free to stroke the head and horn of the sleeping creature and absorb good luck from it.

A rather more drastic method of capture, mentioned in numerous medieval texts, was to get a unicorn riled up enough to attack. This was not easy with such a serene creature, but if you were successful you were advised to stand in front of a stout tree and hold your ground as the enraged unicorn charged. At the last possible moment, just before you were skewered, you should jump aside. The unicorn's momentum would drive its horn into the tree trunk and it would become stuck there. This was the tactic Shakespeare had in mind when he had the character Decius Brutus say in *Julius Caesar*, "he loves to hear that unicorns may be betray'd with trees."

*

The horn of the unicorn has consistently been its most famous feature, its source of magic, and its undoing. For hundreds of years any pharmacy worth its Epsom salts carried a supply of powdered unicorn horn, and it was a rare person of power and wealth who did not own at least one horn. Swirling the horn in muddy water was said to clear the water and purify it; immersing the horn in a draft of poison could make the liquid safe to drink. Ground to a powder and ingested, the horn was believed to act as a powerful aphrodisiac and to cure impotence, infertility, epilepsy, plague, and other ailments. A sixteenth-century advertisement by a London doctor claimed that an elixir of his own concoction, after being run through a unicorn horn, could cure "Scurvy, Old Ulcers, Dropsie, Running Gout, Consumptions, Distillations, Coughs, Palpitation of the Heart, Fainting Fits, Convulsions, Kings Evil, Rickets in Children, Melancholly or Sadness, The Green Sickness, Obstructions, and all Distempers proceeding from a Cold Cause."

Where there is a market, there will always be a supply. Entrepreneurs traveled the world in search of unicorns, and when they failed to find them, they improvised. During the Middle Ages and the Renaissance, the horns of antelopes and rhinoceroses were often sold as genuine unicorn horn, or alicorn. By far the most common substitute was the tusk of the narwhal, a cetacean found only in the Arctic Ocean. In the male of this species, one of its two canine teeth protrudes through its lip and grows into a long, spiraled tusk that can reach a length of nine feet and is similar in appearance to the classic unicorn horn. Since it was so long assumed that every land animal was represented by a corresponding marine animal, the existence of the narwhal, or sea-unicorn, was seen as proof of the existence of a land unicorn. The sea-unicorn was likewise believed to possess magical properties. When British explorer Martin Frobisher returned from his expedition to the Arctic in 1577, he brought with him a six-foot-long tusk that he had found on a dead "sea-unicorn." He tested the tusk's medical potency by placing spiders inside it. When the spiders died, he declared the horn effective in neutralizing poison, and presented it as a gift to Queen Elizabeth I. The queen had previously paid 10,000 pounds for another sea-unicorn horn—about the price you would expect to pay for a mid-sized castle in those days. She was so impressed with Frobisher's gift that she ordered it preserved with the British crown jewels.

Monarchs and popes were long accustomed to paying large sums for narwhal tusks and other bogus horns. Mary Queen of Scots owned one, Philip II of Spain owned twelve, and Frederick III of Denmark sat on a throne made of alicorn. James I of England handed over 10,000 pounds sterling for what he was convinced was a unicorn horn, while Pope Paul III paid 12,000 pieces of gold for another. Such prices were not paid just for esthetic value. In the Middle Ages, assassination by poisoning was greatly feared, and it was believed that any liquid poured into a flask of alicorn would be made safe. Food could be cleansed of poison merely by touching the horn.

In 1746, the English medical establishment finally announced that unicorn horn was an ineffective medicine. But it wasn't until the early nineteenth century that most people began to doubt the existence of unicorns themselves, thanks largely to a published report by the French naturalist Georges Cuvier. He wrote in 1827 that unicorns could not exist because mammals with cloven hooves had skulls divided down the center and a horn could not grow from such a division. The value of alicorn went into steep decline and the animal's credibility faded.

Lewis Carroll is one of many authors who have given modern-day fans of unicorns some hope for their existence. In *Through the Looking Glass*, a unicorn sees Alice for the first time and asks in amazement, "What—is—this?" Informed that it is a child, the unicorn says, "I always thought they were fabulous monsters." Alice, in turn, admits that she had always assumed unicorns were imaginary. Like a parent protecting a child from disillusionment, the unicorn offers a reasonable proposition. "If you'll believe in me," he says, "I'll believe in you."

28
DINOSAUR HUNTING
IN OUR TIME

Something in us wants to believe in dragons. When my brother and I were kids we watched a film version of Arthur Conan Doyle's *The Lost World* and afterward went outside to search for dinosaurs. In the neglected valley across the road from our house we found them, or their tracks anyway: strange, plate-sized depressions spaced too widely to be made by any animal we knew, crossing the otherwise undisturbed surface of a sandy washout. The tracks could have been left by a running human, I suppose, could even have been left by my brother or me, but we were convinced we were on the trail of a *Stegosaurus* or a *Tyrannosaurus* (a young one, its teeth not fully formed). We were determined to capture the sucker, so we began digging a trap-pit but soon gave up because there were too many rocks. Following the tracks seemed like a good strategy until we lost them in an aspen thicket. Then we bent stout saplings to make snares but couldn't figure out a good triggering mechanism. Life has never been easy for dinosaur hunters.

My brother and I were not the first to be prodded to action by

Professor Challenger's isolated South American plateau and its population of remnant dinosaurs. Shortly after publication of Conan Doyle's novel in 1912, newspapers reported that a group of explorers in a yacht owned by the University of Pennsylvania had set out on a voyage up the Amazon in search of a lost world. Conan Doyle was not particularly impressed that the explorers had taken his book seriously. "Let 'em go!" he reportedly said. "If they don't find the plateau, they'll certainly find *something* of interest."

The lost-world scenario has been around since at least 1801, when French paleontologist Georges Cuvier proposed that the extinction of species was a fact of life. Because extinction seemed to contradict the Bible, other scientists of Cuvier's time proposed that the fossil bones then being excavated in France, Germany, and England were the remains of animals that had disappeared from Europe but not from remote and unexplored regions of the world. Cuvier was skeptical. He thought it unlikely that any large animals could have gone unnoticed by explorers.

But others seized upon the idea with enthusiasm. Thomas Jefferson, who was fascinated with Cuvier's new science of paleontology, conjectured that the Lewis and Clark expedition might find relic populations of presumed-extinct mammals in the vast American West. In 1803, he wrote in a letter: "It happens that we are now actually sending off a small party to explore the Missouri to its source... It is not improbable that this voyage of discovery will procure us further information of the Mammoth and the Megatherium also... we had found here some remains of an enormous animal incognitum, whom, from the disproportionate length of his claw, we had denominated Megalonxy, and which is probably the same animal; and that there are symptoms of its late and present existence. The route we are exploring will perhaps bring us further evidence of it."

Were Jefferson alive today he might well be a member of a small, colorful band of scientists and pseudo-scientists who call themselves cryptozoologists. The name, derived from the Greek *kryptos*, for hidden or secret, translates to "the science of hidden animals." It was coined in the

1950s by French biologist Bernard Heuvelmans, author of *On the Track of Unknown Animals* and *In the Wake of the Sea-Monsters*. As founder in 1982 of the International Society of Cryptozoology (ISC), Heuvelmans defined his science as "The scientific study of hidden animals, i.e., of still unknown animal forms about which only testimonial and circumstantial evidence is available, or material evidence considered insufficient by some." Among the best-known "cryptids" (as the ISC calls them) that Heuvelmans and his followers seek to study are abominable snowmen, Bigfoot, the Loch Ness monster, and various serpents and monsters of the seas.

Less well-known are creatures such as the tatzelwurm, a short, stumpy, lizardlike dweller of burrows and caves in the Swiss, Bavarian, and Austrian Alps. Though a specimen has never been captured or found dead, their legend lives on. Naturalist Friedreich von Tschuki described the tatzelwurm in 1861 as "a sort of 'cave-worm' which is thick, three to six feet long, and has two short legs; it appears at the approach of storms after a long dry spell... Many honest and respectable people swear that they have seen it with their own eyes." If the creature exists it is likely that it is related to the worm lizards, skinks, and other burrowing lizards. A specimen said to have been found in 1828 was partially eaten by a crow and the skeleton was lost in transit while being sent to zoologists for identification. A photograph published to great acclaim in German newspapers in 1934 shows a short, squat, ferociously toothed creature that appears to be made of papier mache.

Another obscure object of crypto-searches is the bunyip of Australia, a barrel-shaped, carnivorous, aquatic mammal said to have the head of a dog, ears of a pig, feet of an emu, and to be the size of a large dog or seal. It has been reported seen in Australian ponds and lagoons for more than 100 years, and appears prominently in aboriginal legends. Cryptozoologists have conjectured that the creature might be an undiscovered species of marsupial or a large relative of the platypus.

Cryptozoologists are intrigued as well by mysterious giant birds they call "thunderbirds" that have been reported for centuries in many places around the world. Descriptions vary widely, from giant owls to massive eagles to *Teratornis merriami*, an extinct relative of the condor that had a twelve-foot wingspan and scavenged the carcasses of mammoths during the ice age. The one characteristic all thunderbirds seem to have in common is the ability to snatch up and carry away humans (usually children) and then disappear before experienced birders have a chance to add them to their life lists.

An advertising blurb for the book, *Extraordinary Animals Worldwide* by Karl Shuker, lists the following crypto-creatures: "The Mono Grande is featured, as are Gulper Eels, snake-stones and serpent kings, blue rhinoceri, the amazing New Guinea Singing Dog, and giant carnivorous terror birds." Another book by Shuker, *Mystery Cats of the World*, includes descriptions of "Surrey pumas, Exmoor beasts, spotted lions, blue bobcats, onzas, Queensland tigers, scimitar cats, and many more."

Cryptozoologists justify their searches for mysterious animals by pointing to the discoveries in relatively recent times of the okapi, the coelacanth, the giant panda, the mountain gorilla, the Komodo dragon, the pygmy hippo, the Congo peacock, the Indo-Chinese forest ox, the king cheetah, and the megamouth shark. Virtually all zoologists agree that there are millions of species—mostly insects—yet to be discovered, named, and studied. Cryptozoologists insist that if conventional scientists opened their minds a little wider they would see that the world might harbor dinosaurs as well.

Rumors of gigantic, reptile-like creatures have surfaced for hundreds of years—thousands of years if you count ancient myths and legends of dragons. Eighteenth-century missionaries reported seeing strange, clawed footprints the size of pie plates in Congo and elsewhere in Africa, and numerous travelers recounted native legends that often spoke of giant, dinosaurlike monsters inhabiting swamps, lakes, and rivers in remote regions of the continent.

In 1919, the *New York Times* reported that a Belgian traveler, a Monsieur Capelle, claimed he had shot at and been chased by an enormous creature he described as "about twenty-four feet in length with a long pointed snout adorned with tusks like horns and a short horn above the nostrils." Though the animal he described sounds a bit like *Triceratops*, the press reported the creature was a brontosaur. Editors were skeptical (the *Times'* headline read "Perhaps He Only Dreamt It"), and, as it turned out, they had good reason to be: The Capelle incident was eventually proven a hoax, but not before rumors circulated that the Smithsonian Institution was offering a reward of a million pounds for the capture, dead or alive, of any brontosaur from Africa. An English war veteran named Leicester Stevens took the rumor seriously enough to launch a highly publicized expedition in search of zoological fame and fortune. He and his dog left for Africa in a blaze of publicity, but returned quietly to England a short time later having seen no animals even remotely like a brontosaur or *Triceratops*.

Over the years there have been persistent hazy reports from Africa's Congo of a saurian monster known as *mokele-mbembe* ("he who stops the flow of rivers"), which figures in the mythology of the region's pygmies. The rumors have inspired several expeditions, the most ambitious of which were undertaken by Roy Mackal, a biologist at the University of Chicago and vice-president of the International Society of Cryptozoology. Mackal first went to Congo in search of dinosaurs in February 1980, in the company of James Powell, a reputed crocodile expert. Mackal and Powell saw no dinosaurs, but they collected a number of intriguing eyewitness accounts from natives. Some described *mokele-mbembe* as a snake-like animal up to fifty feet long, with a head sporting a crown similar to a rooster's comb, and a long, sinuous tail. Others described creatures that fit the description of sauropods, those immense herbivorous Jurassic dinosaurs.

Equipped with cameras and sonar equipment, Mackal returned the following year with J. Richard Greenwell, secretary of ISC, and Marcellin Agnagna. They again failed to find *mokele-mbembe*, although once, coming around the bend of a river in their canoes, they were pitched in the wake of a large, unseen animal that had just submerged and that they were sure was neither a hippo nor a crocodile. In 1983 Agnagna mounted an expedition of his own into the heart of the vast swamp named Likouala, where sightings of the *mokele-mbembe* were most common, and reported seeing a distinctly dinosaurian animal "with a wide back, a long neck, and small head" surface in front of him. Unfortunately, the zoologist was too startled to take photos.

Cryptozoologists offer various explanations for the existence of mysterious animals. Some insist cryptids are undiscovered species or relics of species thought to be extinct. Others, like John Mitchell and Robert J. M. Rickard in their book *Living Wonders*, argue for a "theory of revivals," which uses the recurrence of similar forms in nature (such as a bear-shaped tree stump in woods once inhabited by bears) to suggest that nature repeats itself so thoroughly that on occasion specimens of even extinct animals can return to existence. Still others have proposed a kind of natural time-and-space travel similar to the "teleportation" of science fiction, which can occasionally drop kangaroos in Ohio, alligators in Manhattan, and dinosaurs in Congo.

As the wild portions of the earth shrink, our hope that they shelter fantastic creatures shrinks with them. Cryptozoologists beseech the rest of us to keep our minds open. The world is mysterious and filled with marvels and for all we know, inhabited by creatures so strange they would make the velociraptors of the *Jurassic Park* films seem fit for a petting zoo.

Personally, I'm so astonished by the existence of sphinx moths and sea otters that I'm satisfied to live in a world without dinosaurs and sasquatches. But I'd be thrilled if someone discovered a *Triceratops* living in Congo. The first thing I'd do is call my brother and ask if he remembers that trail we followed—and lost—so many years ago.

29
REALLY, REALLY
AMAZING ANIMALS

When I was fourteen years old, some older guys in the neighborhood invited me to join them on a hunting expedition. They said that if I waited at the end of my driveway at sundown with hip waders, a flashlight, and a fishing net, they would pick me up and drive me to the woods and show me how to capture the elusive, wary snipe.

I was already familiar with a snipe of a different feather, Wilson's snipe, *Gallinago delicata,* a relative of the woodcock and the sandpipers. I knew from my Peterson's field guide that this snipe could be found sitting tight in bogs all across northern North America. Not the same critter, said the guys. The real snipe, they said, was a mammal about the size of a hamster, a cute fuzzball so shy you almost never saw it. Anyone lucky enough to catch one could cage it and make it into a pet.

"So, you wanna go?" they asked.

I was flattered to be asked, but the story aroused a snipelike wariness in me. Good thing. If I had gone along with the plan, I would have been led into a forest, told to shut off my flashlight and in the darkness chant

"Snipe! Snipe! Snipe!" until one of the creatures sidled up and I could scoop it into my net.

Of course no snipe would have appeared. By the time I switched my light back on, my guides would have disappeared and I would have had to walk home alone along dark roads, feeling like an idiot.

American folklore is filled with imaginary creatures designed to hoodwink gullible greenhorns. These creatures hold a special place in the bestiary of the world's fabulous, legendary, and mythical animals. Unlike unicorns and dragons, few were actually thought to exist. Unlike with Bigfoot, Yeti, and the Loch Ness Monster, no expeditions have been launched in search of them. Yet, for several hundred years these mythic animals have been lively inhabitants of our national lore and the source of much entertainment and a fair amount of confusion.

Many uniquely American creatures can be traced to lumbermen, sailors, cowboys, miners, and other working-class storytellers. During the nineteenth and early twentieth centuries, lumberjacks from Maine to Oregon found the woods alive with strange creatures such as the axehandle hound (which resembled a dachshund, but with a head shaped like a hatchet, and with an appetite for wooden axe handles), the agropelter (a tree-top dweller that caused deadly limbs to fall on woodcutters), the teakettler (best known for its high-pitched call, which sounded like a boiling teakettle; witnesses say it walked backward and emitted clouds of vapor from its mouth), the goofus bird (which always flew backwards and built its nests upside down), the squonk (so morose that it could be tracked by following the stream of tears it left behind during its constant weeping), and the upland trout (which flew rapidly among the tree tops and was afraid of water).

Among the most frequently discussed animals was the sidehill gouger, a mammal with long legs on one side of its body and short legs on the other, an adaptation that allowed it to keep an even keel while traversing steep hillsides. It was also know as the sidehill hoofer, sidehill wowser, sidehill guano, yamhill lunkus, rackabore, wampus cat, and mountain stem-winder. Gougers were dangerous when confronted face-to-face—

some were armed with a drill-like snout that allowed them to burrow rapidly underground or through the sides of a log cabin—but if you happened to meet one on a hillside, all you had to do to avoid an attack was take a step up or down the hill.

In Texas, the sidehill gouger was known as the gwinther. Once, some cowboys tried to capture one as it ran around a mountain. They noticed that it climbed a little higher with each lap, so they reasoned that the best way to catch it was to wait until it reached the peak and had nowhere to go. But when the gwinther got to the top of the mountain, it turned inside out and ran back around the opposite way, going lower with every circuit.

In some tales, the gouger was a large, fierce, catlike predator that preyed on humans. In another version, it was the size of a calf and looked rather like a beaver. It laid eggs the size of buckets, each big enough to provide breakfast for twenty-five lumbermen. Maine had two subspecies, the sidehill winder, which circled hills in a counterclockwise direction, and sidehill unwinder, which traveled clockwise. If the two happened to meet head-on, they fought fiercely, neither willing (or able) to yield.

If a sidehill gouger happened to fall over, it would lie helpless until it died of starvation. In Arkansas, its carcass became food for the baldknob buzzard, a giant vulture with only a single wing, which could fly in one direction only and thus spent its entire life circling the same hilltop.

The hugag was another creature that got in trouble when it fell over. It resembled a moose in size and appearance, but its legs lacked joints, forcing the animal to spend its entire life standing. Because its lower lip was so long, the hugag could not graze on the ground but had to feed on twigs and branches.

In his 1910 book *Fearsome Creatures of the Lumberwoods, with a Few Desert and Mountain Beasts*, Minnesota forester William T. Cox described a hugag from lumber camps of the nineteenth century:

> It is reported to keep going all day long, browsing on twigs,
> flopping its lip around trees, and stripping bark as occasion offers,
> and at night, since it cannot lie down, it leans against a tree, bracing

its hind legs and marking time with its front ones. The most successful hugag hunters have adopted the practice of notching trees so that they are almost ready to fall, and when the hugag leans up against one both the tree and the animal come down.

The hugag's genealogy is ancient. Compare the above description with this one written more than 1,900 years ago by Pliny the Elder: "… the achlis, born in the island of Scandinavia…has no joint at the hock and consequently is unable to lie down but sleeps leaning against a tree, and is captured by the tree being cut through to serve as a trap…Its upper lip is exceptionally big; on account of this it walks backward when grazing, so as to avoid getting tripped up by it in moving forward."

The Animal That Can't Lie Down became a familiar character in the medieval bestiaries and was later described in colonists' tales in early America. By the time lumberjacks began spinning yarns, it played a standard role in many storytellers' repertoires.

Another standard was the hoopsnake, which during the colonial period was widely believed to exist in nature. Various accounts claimed the snake to be aggressive and deadly. It attacked enemies and escaped predators by grasping its tail in its mouth to form a circle and rolling across the ground at high speed. The hoopsnake was armed with a spur or stinger loaded with venom so deadly that should it slam into a tree while rolling the tree would lose its leaves and die. If you needed to defend yourself against a hoopsnake you had to bear in mind that striking it with a stick was perilous: The snake's powerful venom might flow up the wood to your arm and kill you. The hoopsnake had foul breath, spit quarts of green poison, traveled in packs of hundreds or millions, and would chase unfortunate people for miles in its determination to sting them. By the nineteenth century, when most people had stopped believing in hoopsnakes, the creature had lodged firmly in the popular imagination and was a favorite subject of yarns and tall tales. Barstool bards still tell the stories, and some listeners may even believe them.

One imaginary creature of the nineteenth century was profitable to hucksters who traveled from town to town. They would post handbills for a showing of "The Monster Guyuscutus" and collect admission from gullible customers. One report described the creature as like a lizard, hatched from eggs the size of beer kegs, twenty feet long, and armed with sharp tusks. Typically, at some point early in the show, while the "monster" raged and rampaged out of sight in the wings, one of the showmen would run onstage, covered with blood, his clothes torn to tatters, and shout that the monster was loose, instigating a panic in the audience. During the commotion that followed, the hucksters would escape. Mark Twain made use of a variation of the story in the "Royal Nonesuch" episode of *Huckleberry Finn*.

The evolutionary ecologist Daniel S. Simberloff has traced the evolution of one of the best-known hoax-animals, the jackalope, a horned rabbit that is featured to this day on countless postcards in the American west. Simberloff wrote in an article in *Natural History* magazine in 1987 that the jackalope was not the invention of tourist boosters in Douglas, Wyoming, a community that has claimed to be the jackalope capital of the world since a local taxidermist named Ralph Herrick concocted the creature from parts of a jackrabbit and a pronghorn, but is instead a mythical creature with a long and varied history across several continents. He found a pair of horned hares nearly identical to the American jackalope in a book of natural curiosities written in 1662 by a Jesuit priest, Gaspar Schott, in what is now Germany. Today, Bavarian shops in that region sell postcards, books, and mounted specimens of the *wolpertinger*, a rabbit or hare bearing the antlers of a deer. Even further afield are ancient tales from Africa that describe rabbits wearing horns made of wax that would melt if the creatures came too near a fire. Simberloff went so far as to uncover a possible biological explanation for jackalopes and their kin. According to him, a virus called papilloma occasionally infects hares, rabbits, and other mammals, causing benign growths that sometimes take the form of hornlike protuberances from the skull. The virus is found in many places, including Africa, central Europe, and the plains of North America.

Stories paint a psychological portrait of the people who tell them.

American folklore is big, bold, colorful, and when we take the stage we tend to be extravagant, imaginative, boastful, and outrageous. It's who we are. We might never see a sidehill gouger or a hoopnake but the folks who talk about them are around us every day and we're happy to hand over a few dollars for the privilege of listening.

I'm sorry that I didn't go out that night in search of the mythical snipe. Something vital and primitive might have been triggered by the search. A snipe is no more fantastic, after all, than a porcupine (armed with barbed spikes!) or an opossum (rolls over and plays dead!) or a skunk (sprays a foul-smelling liquid from its butt!). It probably would have done me some good to spend a night in the woods, in the dark, my heart full of hope and wonder, chanting, "Snipe! Snipe! Snipe!"

30
PLINY'S WORLD OF WONDERS

My grandmother was afraid of snakes. There's nothing unusual about that, of course, but Grandma's fear went deep. She believed that snakes are malicious and that if you kill one even in self-defense its mate will track you down and take vengeance. She also believed snakes drink milk from cows. She said that when she was a child in New Jersey, a neighbor who was worried about his cow's sudden loss of productivity spent the night in the barn expecting to catch a thief and watched with his own eyes as a snake twined up the cow's hind leg, latched onto an udder, and sucked poor Bessie dry.

I said, "Grandma, that myth is as old as the hills. Pliny the Elder described the same thing almost 2,000 years ago."

"See?" she said, raising an eyebrow at my insolence. "Proof!"

My grandmother never read Pliny—had never even heard of him—but from the first century A.D. through the Renaissance he was one of Western civilization's most influential writers. By the Middle Ages his encyclopedia of the physical world, *Natural History*, was the medieval equivalent of a runaway best-seller, and Pliny was undisputed as an authority on science, nature, mankind, and the cosmos.

In a preface addressed to the emperor Titus, Pliny explained that his purpose in writing *Natural History* was no less than "setting forth in detail all the contents of the entire world." Accomplishing that ambitious feat required him to gather information by the cartload. No subject was too large for him and no detail too small. He synthesized much of what was known in first-century Rome about astronomy, meteorology, geography, anthropology, zoology, botany, pharmacology, mineralogy, and the arts of sculpting and painting—referencing some 2,000 volumes by at least 100 authors to come up with the "20,000 noteworthy facts" he claimed were packed into the thirty-seven books of his encyclopedia.

Those thirty-seven books offer a great deal of very strange reading. If you plow straight through, as I did during a two-week marathon, you find yourself slipping into a slightly altered state of consciousness. Be warned, however: large sections of *Natural History* are a trudge. You might want to avoid Books III, IV, V, and VI, for instance. They deal with the geography of the world in Pliny's time and are composed largely of meticulous and seemingly endless lists of the names of harbors, islands, mountains, rivers, towns, and cities, most of which cannot be found in modern atlases. But even Pliny's dullest pages of reportage are brightened by occasional startling insights and bizarre observations. Throughout the entire encyclopedia, vivid descriptions of the fantastic, fallacious, and unfounded are so boldly juxtaposed with accurate observations and historical and scientific verities that a reader can be forgiven for sometimes confusing the facts and the fallacies.

The fallacies alone are worth the price of admission. Odd and sensational excerpts from *Natural History* have been so freely copied, pilfered, and plagiarized that some of them still linger in our legends, superstitions, folklore, and mythologies. Do porcupines shoot their quills in self-defense? No, but Pliny wrote that the animal "pierces the mouths of hounds when they close with it, and shoots out at them when further off," and the idea is still one of the most widespread zoological myths. Do our ears ring when we're the subject of gossip? There's no reason they should, but Pliny gave sanction to that bit of lore when he said it was an "accepted belief" that "absent people can divine by the ringing in their ears that they are the object of talk." Do hair and fingernails grow on a corpse? Pliny mentioned in passing that they do, and a hundred generations of boys and girls have repeated the story with delicious shudders of horror.

In his calm, authoritative voice, Pliny assures readers that various parts of the world are home to dog-headed people who communicate by barking; fast-running people whose feet are turned backwards and have sixteen toes; a tribe of one-legged people who get around by hopping at great speed and whose single foot is so large that on hot days they lie on their backs with their foot in the air shading them like an umbrella. Furthermore, he says, there are neckless people with eyes in their shoulders; mouthless people who draw all of their nourishment from the scent of roots, flowers, and apples and can be killed by offensive odors; and people who are seven and a half feet tall, never spit, are exempt from toothaches and headaches and can stare all day at the sun without harm.

The animal kingdom is equally fantastic. In ancient Paeonia (probably in what is now Macedonia) was an animal called the "bonasus" that might have been the now extinct aurochs, though Pliny's description gave it defensive capabilities seen in few animals: "[It] has the mane of a horse but in all other respects resembles a bull; its horns are curved back in such a manner as to be of no use for fighting, and it is said that because of this it saves itself by running away, meanwhile emitting a trail of dung that sometimes covers a distance of as much as three furlongs, contact with which scorches pursuers like a sort of fire."

In India there is the "mantichora," a terrifying carnivore with the body of a lion, the face and ears of a man, grey eyes, a triple row of teeth, and a scorpion-like tail that can inflict horrible stings. Blood-red in color, it runs at great speed, sings in a voice that sounds like a pan-pipe blended with a trumpet, and has "a special appetite for human flesh."

Equally fearsome is the Indian unicorn, with its horselike body, head of a stag, feet of an elephant, tail of a boar, and a single black horn three feet long projecting from the middle of its forehead—an animal that calls in a deep bellow and is so fierce when threatened that it can never be captured alive.

The "basilisk serpent" of Africa kills bushes on contact, bursts rocks with its scorching breath, and is so venomous that when a man on horseback killed one, "the infection rising through the spear killed not only the rider but also the horse."

In Pliny's pantheon of wildlife even many recognizable animals possess fabulous powers. Snakes wait in ambush in tall grass and launch themselves into the sky to intercept high-flying birds. Other snakes grow so large that they prey on elephants and can swallows bulls whole. Hyenas are hermaphroditic, capable of alternating sexes year by year, and are such gifted mimics that at night they prey on shepherds by calling their names to lure them out of their cabins. Elephants possess the virtues of honesty, wisdom, justice, and reverence for the sun and moon, and are nearly as intelligent as humans. Those elephants too slow-witted to master tricks can be found practicing alone at night until they learn to climb ropes and write simple messages in Greek. All elephants, smart or dim-witted, "hate the mouse worst of living creatures, and if they see one merely touch the fodder placed in their stall they refuse it with disgust."

Pliny assures us that the mating habits of animals are bizarre and often inexplicable. To breed horses, for instance, "It is known that… mares when a west wind is blowing stand facing towards it and conceive the breath of life and that this produces a foal, and this is the way to breed a very swift colt." Goats are "hotter in coupling" than sheep because "…they breathe through the ears, not the nostrils, and are never free from fever." Snakes mate by embracing tightly until "the male viper inserts its head into the female viper's mouth, and the female is so enraptured with pleasure that she gnaws it off." The twentieth-century Italian novelist Italo Calvino was captivated by Pliny's zoology and sensed a kindred spirit at work. He concluded that Pliny's uncritical mixing of the practical and the fabulous added up to nothing less than "a guided tour of the human imagination."

Pliny was born Gaius Plinius Secundus in A.D. 23 in the town of Como in northern Italy. Almost nothing is known of his early life, but it is likely that his parents had fairly high social standing, were comfortably wealthy, and had ambitions for their son to climb in the social and political worlds of the Roman Empire. First in Como and later in Rome, he was educated in science, philosophy, literature, art, theater, and oratory. At the age of twenty-three he entered the military and served most of his seven or eight years of duty as an officer in Germany, where he rose in rank to commander of an auxiliary cavalry regiment. After his military service he returned to Rome to study law and pursue a literary career.

Most of the details known about Pliny's life and career have survived in eloquent letters written by his nephew, Pliny the Younger. They portray the elder Pliny as a man of intense curiosity and ambition, so tireless in his research and so dedicated to the life of letters that he slept only a few hours each day, devoted virtually every waking moment to his work and in the fifty-six years that he lived, tallied the equivalent of several lifetimes' worth of accomplishments. In addition to being a scholar and writer, he was a soldier, lawyer, government administrator, and personal advisor to an emperor. "You will wonder," Pliny the Younger wrote, "how a man so engaged as he was, could find time to compose such a number of books." It helped, apparently, that he was gifted with "quick apprehension, incredible zeal, and a wakefulness beyond compare," and that he adhered religiously to a strict and disciplined system of managing his time.

The key to that system was to never waste a minute. Pliny typically worked about twenty hours out of every twenty-four. He began his day at midnight or one in the morning, studying and writing until shortly before dawn, when he would leave home to meet with the emperor

Vespasian and spend several hours attending to matters of state. After he had fulfilled those obligations, he returned home by chariot or sedan chair, taking notes as a servant read to him, and worked the remainder of the morning. At noon he ate a light lunch, and, when the weather was pleasant, rested for a short time outside in the sun listening as books were read to him. He then bathed in cold water, napped, and went back to work until dinner. Even as he ate he jotted notes and listened as books were read aloud to him. No information was without profit, and no moment could be spared. He once saw his nephew taking a leisurely stroll and chastised him for wasting time that he could have spent reading or writing.

Only *Natural History* and a few fragments of Pliny's other books have survived, but it is clear that his literary output was astonishing by any standard. According to a letter by his nephew, Pliny's first book was *The Art of Using a Javelin on Horseback*, written while he was in the cavalry in Germany. It was followed by *The Life of Pomponius Secundus*, a two-volume memorial to the senator who probably helped him secure his first military posting. His third undertaking was an ambitious one: *The History of the Wars in Germany*, a twenty-volume account of Rome's military campaigns against the German tribes, a project Pliny claimed was inspired by a dream in which the ghost of a Roman soldier came to him and requested his memory be preserved in text. It was followed by *The Students*, a six-volume treatise on the art of oratory; *Linguistic Queries*, an eight-volume scholarly work; and a one-volume update to a thirty-volume history of Rome, *History of Our Own Times*. There were, in addition, 160 volumes of unpublished notebooks. But Pliny's crowning achievement, finished in A.D. 77, two years before his death, was *Natural History*.

Pliny's magnum opus fits into the tradition of a long line of handbooks of knowledge meant to be primarily compendia of information. The bulk of that information was compiled from the work of other authors. In his quest for knowledge, Pliny plundered all available sources, from hearsay and travelers' tales to the evidence of his own senses, but the best plunder by far came from the library. Learned borrowings were a standard feature of ancient scholarship. Roman authors loved to pare down, digest, and simplify the words of other thinkers and writers. In many cases, it is the popularizers of scholarship who are known to us today, rather than the originators of it, since works written for general readers were more widely dispersed and more often copied and therefore had a better chance of surviving than esoteric and technical works. Plagiarism, not surprisingly, was rampant. In typical fashion, Aristotle's *Meteorologica* was the primary source for Posidonius' book about meteorology, *Peri meteoron*. Posidonius' book has not survived but it was central to Seneca's *Natural Questions* and was relied on extensively by Lucretius in his *On the Nature of the Universe.*

Aristotle was an important reference for Pliny, as well, though certainly not the only one. Like the authors before him, Pliny borrowed heavily from many sources, but contrary to common practice, he listed his authorities and gave them credit where it was due. He went to that trouble, he wrote, because it is honorable "to own up to those who were the means of one's achievements, not to do as most of the authors to whom I have referred did. For you must know that when collating authorities I have found that the most professedly reliable and modern writers have copied the old authors word for word, without acknowledgement."

Many of the handbooks and encyclopedias of antiquity were unavoidably dull, a shortcoming Pliny avoided by spicing his facts with commentary, making for more interesting reading and, perhaps unintentionally, revealing glimpses of the author's personality. From the clues offered by dozens of brief essays on subjects as disparate as the declining moral values of Romans, the shameful quackery of the medical profession, and the importance of nurturing the natural environment, we learn that Pliny was practical, pragmatic, moralistic, and opinionated. He was surely a man of his times, a Roman through and through, proud of his citizenship and convinced of the precedence of the empire over the individual. He was a stoic with no illusions about human weakness and unreliability. He accepted the existence of fabulous creatures, but was skeptical of magic and astrology, remained a trusting devotee of a benevolent and maternal Earth but stayed aloof from a deity he believed had little interest in humanity. He was, above all, curious about everything.

Although his interests were broad, Pliny was clearly more captivated by some subjects than others. He composed most of *Natural History* in a simple, unadorned style, yet broke into near-song when describing certain natural wonders.

About the moon, for instance, he wrote: "…she has racked the wits of observers, who are ashamed that the star which is nearest should be the one about which we know least—always waxing and waning, and now curved into the horns of a sickle, now just halved in size, now rounded into a circle; spotted and then suddenly shining clear; vast and full-orbed, and then all of a sudden not there at all."

On insects: "Where did Nature find a place in a flea for all the senses? …at what point in its surface did she place sight? Where did she attach taste? Where did she insert smell? …But we marvel at elephants' shoulders carrying castles, and bulls' necks and the fierce tossings of their heads, at the rapacity of tigers and the manes of lions, whereas really Nature is to be found in her entirety nowhere more than in her smallest creations."

On human eyes: "…the eyes are the abode of the mind. They glow, stare, moisten, wink; from them flows the tear of compassion, when we kiss them we seem to reach the mind itself, they are the source of tears and of the stream that bedews the cheek."

On Earth: "She belongs to men as the sky belongs to God: she receives us at birth, and gives us nurture after birth, and when once brought forth she upholds us always, and at the last when we have now been disinherited by the rest of nature she embraces us in her bosom and at the very time gives us her maternal shelter… Water rises in mist, freezes into hail, swells in waves, falls headlong in torrents; air becomes thick with clouds and rages with storms; but Earth is kind and gentle and indulgent, ever a handmaid in the service of mortals, producing under our compulsion, or lavishing of her own accord, what scents and savours, what juices, what surfaces for the touch, what colours!"

On the music of the spheres: "Whether the sound of this vast mass whirling in unceasing rotation is of enormous volume and consequently beyond the capacity of our ears to perceive, for my part I cannot easily say—any more in fact than whether this is true of the tinkling of the stars that travel round with it, revolving in their own orbits; or whether it emits a sweet harmonious music that is beyond belief charming. To us who live within it, the world glides silently alike by day and night."

If Pliny was a poet, he was a very practical one. Much of *Natural History* reads like an ancient version of *The Farmer's Almanac*, offering answers to problems people encountered in their daily lives, especially in garden, orchard, and farmyard. Pliny's discourses on raising bees, cultivating grape vines, harvesting figs, preserving fruits, and producing linen from flax are as specific and accurate as those in modern guidebooks to rural life. On subjects about which he had personal experience, he flat-out knew his stuff. Onions, for instance: "Those of the roundest shape are the best; also a red onion is more pungent than a white one, or a dry one than one still fresh, and a raw one than one that has been cooked." At his most practical, Pliny wrote a prose that could serve as a model of precision and economy: "Boiling oxhide produces glue; bull's hide makes the best."

The encyclopedia's practical applications have contributed much to its popularity through the centuries. The books on drugs and home remedies for illness and disease were frequently printed in a separate edition, *Medicina Plinii*, which probably first appeared in about the fourth century and is known to have been reprinted at least as late as 1509. The appeal of that volume is sometimes difficult to understand. Pliny's treatments for headache included crushing snails and rubbing them on the forehead, applying an ointment made from the brain of a vulture to the inner part of the nostrils, eating boiled crow or owl brains, and wrapping the temples with a rope that had been used in a suicide. If those don't ease a headache, try "the head of a snail cut off with a

reed as he feeds in the morning, by preference when the moon is full…
attached in a linen cloth by a thread to the head of the sufferer." For
toothache he advised rinsing the teeth in a solution of vinegar and boiled
frogs. Sneezing and hiccoughs could be stopped by kissing the nose of
a mule. For stomach-ache, lay a puppy across your belly. To cure hair
loss, dandruff, and "scanty eyebrows" rub with an ointment made from
bull urine mixed with sulfur. Anyone unfortunate enough to swallow a
leech should drink vinegar. More familiar and palatable is this treatment
for a dazzling variety of maladies: "Chicken broth also, taken by the
mouth, is a splendid remedy, being wonderfully good for… prolonged
fevers, paralyzed and palsied limbs, diseases of the joints, headaches, eye-
fluxes, flatulence, loss of appetite, incipient tenesmus, complaints of liver,
kidneys, and bladder, indigestion, and asthma."

As Earth was explored and science began making significant progress
in the sixteenth and seventeenth centuries, *Natural History* began to lose
credibility. Attacks against it began appearing as early as 1492, with the
publication of "Concerning the Errors of Pliny" by Italian physician and
scholar Niccoló Leoniceno. By the end of the seventeenth century his
work had been discounted by most of the influential Western scientific
thinkers. Today he is remembered primarily for his mistakes.

But he was not always mistaken. Portions of his sections on botany,
mineralogy, and metallurgy have earned Pliny the praise of modern
experts for being comprehensive and correct. And though he was certainly
an uncritical and often careless researcher, in a number of passages Pliny
proved he could be a perceptive observer. He noticed, as many people
have not, that rainbows only occur opposite the sun, and "high in the sky
when the sun is low and low when it is high." Discussing the electrical
phenomenon now called St. Elmo's Fire, he wrote, "I have seen a radiance
of star-like appearance clinging to the javelins of soldiers on sentry duty
at night in front of the rampart; and on a voyage stars alight on the yards
and other parts of the ship, with a sound resembling a voice, hopping
from perch to perch in the manner of birds."

His description of a nightingale's song is immediate and evocative, as if he composed it while the bird sang just outside his window: "The sound is given out with modulations, and now is drawn out into a long note with one continuous breath, now varied by managing the breath, now made staccato by checking it, or linked together by prolonging it, or carried on by holding it back; or it is suddenly lowered, and at times sinks to a mere murmur, loud, low, bass, treble, with trills, with long notes, modulated when this seems good—soprano, mezzo, baritone; and briefly all the devices in that tiny throat which human science has devised with all the elaborate mechanisms of the flute…"

Of all Pliny's writings, the most interesting might have been a journal entry, now lost, that described the eruption of Mount Vesuvius on August 24, in the year 79. His nephew wrote in a letter to the historian Tacitus that Pliny was working as usual that day in a villa on the shore of the Bay of Naples, where he had been placed in command of a navy fleet sent to suppress pirates. He took his customary sunbath, then a cold bath in water, and ate lunch. He was at work in his study when, at about one o'clock in the afternoon, an unusual cloud down the bay was brought to his attention by his sister, Pliny the Younger's mother. He climbed to the top of a nearby hill to view the cloud, which from that distance was shaped like a pine tree, with broad lateral branches extending from a tall trunk that appeared to grow from Mount Vesuvius.

Pliny wanted a closer look and ordered a small boat prepared. Before the boat could be launched, however, a message arrived from a friend who lived near Vesuvius. She and her family were in fear for their lives and pleaded for rescue. Pliny immediately ordered a fleet of large galleys launched, boarded one himself and ordered it steered toward the city of Stabiae at the base of the volcano.

As his galley crossed the bay, cinders and chunks of pumice fell in such quantities that the captain of the ship urged retreat. Declaring that "fortune befriends the brave," Pliny ordered the fleet to continue on its course, and stood on the open deck watching the volcano and dictating his observations to a secretary. It would be his final literary endeavor.

Pliny reached Stabiae that evening and made his way to his friend's villa. He embraced her and assured her and the others who had gathered in the house that there was no cause for alarm. As if to put everyone at ease, he bathed and ate a cheerful dinner and went to bed early, sleeping so soundly that his snores resounded through the house. The others sat up all night. By morning, so much volcanic debris had fallen that there was danger of being trapped indoors. Pliny and his companions tied pillows over their heads for protection and stepped outside into the rain of stone and ash. Though it should have been light out, the day was enveloped in darkness. They found their way to the shore, but waves prevented them from launching their boats. They had no recourse but to wait for the wind to shift.

Pliny, who was overweight and perhaps suffered from asthma, sat down to rest on a spare sail. When flames and sulfurous gases suddenly swept down onto the beach, everyone but Pliny ran in panic. Two of his slaves tried to help him to his feet, but he fell and they were unable to rouse him. His body was found the next morning, "entire and uninjured…its posture that of a sleeping, rather than a dead man." Pliny the Younger theorized that "some unusually gross vapor…obstructed his breathing and blocked his windpipe, which was not only naturally weak and constricted, but chronically inflamed."

In compiling everything known about natural history in his time, Pliny left an extraordinary record of how he and his contemporaries viewed themselves and their world. It remains a valuable source of information—and sometimes the *only* source of information—about literature, art, science, medicine, agriculture, and lifestyles of the ancient Romans. It was almost certainly a familiar text in the libraries of Marco Polo, Michel de Montaigne, Shakespeare, Milton, and many others who shaped Western culture. In his history of the Roman Empire, Edward Gibbon gave grudging tribute to *Natural History* as "that immense register where Pliny deposited the discoveries, the arts, and the errors of mankind."

The errors, unfortunately, are more famous than the discoveries and arts, and it is tempting to dismiss Pliny outright for being naïve and scientifically inept. After all, as my grandmother was pleased to learn, this was the man who reported that at least one species of snake feeds on "milk sucked from a cow," and who claimed that snakes roam in couples, and if either of them is killed, "the other is incredibly anxious for revenge: it pursues the murderer and by means of some mark of recognition attacks him and him only in however large a throng of people, bursting through all obstacles and traversing all distances, and it is only debarred by rivers or by very rapid flight."

But as a monument to human interpretations of nature and a celebration of our diverse and bountiful planet, *Natural History* continues to inform and entertain. The most enduring of its qualities may simply be the author's tremendous capacity for wonder. His vitality, his enthusiasm, his passion to know and embrace all things equally are refreshing and infectious. "In the contemplation of nature," he wrote, "nothing can possibly be deemed superfluous." The world according to Pliny is overflowing with wonders, both great and small, where everything is interesting and nothing is inconceivable.

ACKNOWLEDGMENTS

Most of the essays and illustrations in this book first appeared, often in quite different form, in *Wildlife Conservation* magazine. We're grateful to executive editor Deborah Behler and art director Julie Larsen Maher for their guidance and encouragement.

Several of the essays also appeared in Grolier's *Science Annuals*. Thanks to editor Joe Castagno, who has remained a good friend and has for many years been a stalwart champion of science education.

"Bellying Up to the World" first appeared in *Wildlife Conservation* and was reprinted in the anthology, *American Nature Writing*.

"The Music of this Sphere" first appeared in *Wildlife Conservation* and was reprinted in *Traverse Magazine*.

"Pliny's World of Wonders" first appeared in *Smithsonian* magazine.

Many family members, friends, and colleagues assisted us during the research and composition of the book. We would especially like to thank Nick Dennis, Aaron and Chelsea Bay Dennis, Gerald and Eva Dennis, Lillie Wolff, Sarah Wolff, Virginia Johnson, Jim and MaryAnn Linsell, and Keith Taylor. As always, we've saved our super extra special thanks for Gail Dennis and Emily Bert.